From Solebay to the Texel: The Third Anglo-Dutch War, 1672-1674

Quintin Barry

'This is the Century of the Soldier', Falvio Testir, Poet, 1641

Helion & Company

Helion & Company Limited
Unit 8 Amherst Business Centre
Budbrooke Road
Warwick
CV34 5WE
England
Tel. 01926 499 619
Fax 0121 711 4075
Email: info@helion.co.uk
Website: www.helion.co.uk
Twitter: @helionbooks
Visit our blog http://blog.helion.co.uk/

Published by Helion & Company 2018
Designed and typeset by Mach 3 Solutions Ltd (www.mach3solutions.co.uk)
Cover designed by Paul Hewitt, Battlefield Design (www.battlefield-design.co.uk)
Printed by Henry Ling Limited, Dorchester, Dorset

Text © Quintin Barry 2018
Images © as individually credited
Maps drawn by George Anderson © Helion & Company 2018

ISBN 978-1-911628-03-3

British Library Cataloguing-in-Publication Data.
A catalogue record for this book is available from the British Library.

For details of other military history titles published by Helion & Company Limited
contact the above address, or visit our website: http://www.helion.co.uk.

We always welcome receiving book proposals from prospective authors.

Contents

List of Illustrations & Maps

Illustrations

Maps

List of Colour Plates

1

The First Anglo-Dutch War

The Anglo-Dutch War which began in 1652 was fought between two countries that might have been supposed to be natural allies rather than enemies. Both were Protestant nations; both had good reason to be wary of the intentions of France and Spain; neither was a monarchy. They had indeed been allied when the Dutch fought the Spanish to gain their independence. For the Commonwealth government in England that followed the ending of the monarchy, a political union with the United Provinces was a logical and realistic policy objective. The Dutch, however, refused to consider this proposal when it was put forward. The immediate cause of this refusal was the suggestion that it would be necessary to banish English Royalist refugees from the United Provinces; the Dutch position was that their country was 'a refuge for the exiles of all nations.'

However, the underlying reasons for this rejection, and for the conflict which ensued, lay in the fierce commercial and financial rivalry between the two nations. Although the English economy had been seriously affected during the years of the Civil War, that had ended with the victory of the commercial and industrial middle classes. Under the Commonwealth the development and expansion of overseas trade had become a central feature of government policy. This was seen as a necessary response to the enormous expansion of Dutch international commerce, which had made Amsterdam the effective capital of a vast trading empire, sustained by the power of its banks and the low interest rates which they offered.

Central to the commercial competition between England and the United Provinces was the effect on the Dutch and English mercantile fleets. For English shipowners, the huge Dutch merchant marine, which could operate far more cheaply thanks to the design of their ships and the fewer crewmen they required, represented a serious threat. So serious was it that in 1651 Parliament felt obliged to intervene, passing into law the Navigation Act which prohibited the import of European goods except in vessels belonging to England or the country of origin, and limiting the import of goods from elsewhere to vessels belonging to England or her colonies. It also required that incoming catches of fish must be by English fishermen, and exports of fish be only in English ships. Similar protectionist legislation had been introduced in past centuries; and measures specifically directed against the Dutch had been enacted in 1624 and 1646.[1]

Legislation of this kind was by no means the only grievance which existed between England and the Dutch Republic. In addition to their strong objections to the Navigation Act, the Dutch challenged the traditional English claim to sovereignty of the seas around the British Isles, which required that all foreign ships should salute English warships by lowering their topsails and flags. The English claim was that by reason of this sovereignty their warships had the right to stop and search foreign vessels that might be carrying cargo destined for any country with which England was in conflict. This included the undeclared maritime war with France that the Commonwealth had been conducting since 1649. The Dutch, not surprisingly, could not accept such a claim, contending that their ships and their cargoes were covered by the Dutch flag, a proposition which they had embodied in a treaty with Spain in 1650. For their part English fishermen found it difficult to compete with the huge Dutch fishing fleets, while English shipowners were disadvantaged by the favourable terms accorded by the King of Denmark to Dutch ships passing through Danish waters into the Baltic. Exception was also taken to the Dutch practice of continuing to trade with the common enemy, as had for instance occurred when the two countries were allied in war against Spain.

It was also regrettably true that the aggressive posture of the English towards the Dutch had its foundation in a strong national dislike, based in part on a feeling that the Dutch had been insufficiently grateful for English support during their war for independence against Spain. The Amboyna massacre of 1623 had also not been forgotten, while the close association between the dispossessed Dutch Stadtholder and the Orange Party and the refugee Stuarts was a further ground for suspicion. Given these influences on popular feeling in England, it would seem that the union between England and the United Provinces which had been proposed by the Commonwealth might in practice have been hard to sell to English public opinion, although whether the man in the street cared as much about the Dutch as historians contend is open to question.

With the passing of the Navigation Act, as well as the continued activity of English privateers in seizing Dutch ships bound for France, which the Commonwealth government allowed to continue unchecked, the status quo was unfavourable to the Dutch. They did not, however, want to have to resort to war. They had everything to lose; the English had everything to gain. The Grand Pensionary, Adriaen Pauw, put the position succinctly: 'The English are about to attack a mountain of gold; we are about to attack a mountain of iron.'[2] The Dutch delegation sent to London in December 1651 to discuss the problems that divided the two countries was set, therefore, an impossible task. The Navigation Act had the greatest impact on Dutch

---

1   Admiral Sir Herbert Richmond, *The Navy as an Instrument of Policy 1558–1727* (Cambridge: Cambridge University Press, 1953), p.97.
2   Roger Hainsworth and Christine Churches, *The Anglo-Dutch Naval Wars 1652–1674* (Stroud: Sutton, 1998), p.17.

Map 1 The North Sea.

commercial interests in the long term; but it was the cessation of the attacks on Dutch shipping which carried the delegation's first priority. Although the negotiations went on at great length, they were, from the Dutch point of view, entirely unproductive. The English had no intention of relinquishing the position of advantage which they occupied.

Confronted by English intransigence, the response of the States General of the United Provinces was to call for the creation of a fleet of 150 warships. This was announced in February 1652. Predictably, it was seen by the Commonwealth government as an explicitly hostile statement of intent. Although, given all the circumstances, the Dutch announcement was understandable, it demanded a strong reaction. Admiral Richmond put it thus:

> In English eyes, and again with equally good reason, this was taken to be an intention to enforce upon England a wholly novel interpretation of the law of nations, an interpretation which would severely hamper her, as a seapower, in the execution of that very act of maritime warfare which constituted the principal weapon: the stoppage of the maritime commerce of an enemy. The right was an old one. It was embodied in the *Consolato del Mare* and had been universally recognised, and the Commonwealth statesmen had no intention of giving way

upon a point which they regarded as vital to the use of the national instrument of warfare.[3]

Unfortunately for the Dutch, however, their shipbuilding programme was far too ambitious. It was simply not feasible to provide a fleet as large as that proposed. At the same time, their existing fleet was inadequate to sustain a prolonged maritime war with England. In any case, ship for ship the Dutch vessels were inferior to those of the English navy; although there were more of them, the English ships were of greater individual strength. The Dutch navy's first priority had been to protect the rich convoys bound to and from the East Indies, so an ability to undertake long cruises was an essential design feature of Dutch warships, but it was also necessary that they be built to traverse their own very shallow home waters. The English fleet, on the other hand, was composed of units developed from the larger and more powerful warships of the fleets of Elizabeth I and James I; speed was seen as less important than individual fighting strength.

The negotiations between the Dutch delegation and the English government dragged on, but the possibility that they might lead to an avoidance of war was minimal. The Dutch procrastinated, and continued to argue for a relaxation of the Navigation Act, and for an end to maritime aggression; for their part, the English demanded prompt replies to the demands which they put forward, which included claims for compensation going back 30 years. The pointlessness of the negotiations deepened the mutual mistrust, which was accentuated by the Dutch plans to enlarge their fleet.

It is fair to say that in the descent to war, the English deserved a large part of the blame. Professor J.R. Jones has referred to the English use of 'naval power in brutal wars of aggression against the Dutch,' going on to write that 'those wars were immoral, economically senseless and best forgotten.'[4] He has also pointed out that the Dutch war aim was the protection of the trade of Holland and Zeeland, and from their perspective, therefore, the Anglo-Dutch wars were entirely defensive. The Dutch saw the English war aim as being no less than the complete domination of the seas, and the consequent total subjection of the Dutch and their trade.

Among the advantages possessed by the English in 1652 was a reformed naval administration which recognised the separate functions of operational command and supply. Overall, the English had the benefit of a unified direction of naval affairs:

> The United Provinces were a federation of seven States with five separate Admiralties. The weakness of government in such a form is a familiar phenomenon. Localism in outlook becomes inevitable. The tendency for each separate territorial unit to relate both expenditure and strategy to what appears to be in its own interest is as marked in national federations as it is in external

---

3   Richmond, p.99.
4   Professor J.R. Jones, *The Anglo-Dutch Wars of the Seventeenth Century* (London: Routledge, 1996), p.5.

alliances. Moreover of the seven Provinces, four had comparatively little interest in foreign commerce, since they had little or no part in it; and so, while a supreme Parliament in London could raise and apply money according to its needs, the States General might call in vain on those Provinces which felt themselves unconcerned in a war. The spirit of localism invaded also the actual conduct of a fleet, causing a lack of cooperation which on some occasions had far reaching harmful effects.[5]

It was in collecting the money necessary to fight the English that the five separate Boards of Admiralty found particular difficulty. The need for additional resources for the Dutch navy was now greater than at any time in Dutch history, but with no unified direction the calls for money fell on deaf ears. Furthermore, the Boards could not in any case provide the ships required of them by the States General:

Their storehouses were sparsely filled in consequence of the general expectation that peace was likely to endure, whilst it was difficult to find a sufficient number of merchant ships to be hired, and it was only by hiring merchant ships that the ships required could be furnished in so short a time. Even if the ships could be acquired, there remained the difficulty of manning them.[6]

The contrast with the situation in England was profound:

In England, however, Parliament was supreme. It could borrow money and assign revenues as it pleased, subject only to the natural limitations on the resources of every government. There were no local boards to complain to a States General representing seven provinces, four of which had little interest in the preservation of commerce in which they had no part.[7]

It was while negotiations were still proceeding between the Dutch delegation and the representatives of the English Council of State that there occurred the first clash between the navies of the two countries. On 12 May 1652, off Start Point, there was an incident between three English warships under the command of Captain Anthony Young and the escort of a Dutch convoy of seven merchantmen from the Mediterranean. Led by Commodore Huyrluyt, who had three warships, the Dutch at first declined to acknowledge English sovereignty by lowering their flags; but after Young sent a boat insisting on this, Huyrluyt, recognising that discretion on this occasion was the better part of valour, complied. The captain of the second escort, Joris van der Zaanen, refused; Young fired a broadside and after the Dutch responded, and a confused engagement took place, van der Zaanen relented and lowered his flag. Young did not persist in a demand that the Dutch commander should surrender and bring his ship into Plymouth.

---

5   Richmond, pp.100–101.
6   Samuel R. Gardiner and C.T. Atkinson (eds.), *Letters and Papers Relating to the First Dutch War* (London: Navy Records Society, 1899), vol. i, p.57.
7   *Ibid.*, p.58.

A week later a more serious incident occurred. As early as 30 April the States General had issued draft instructions to Lieutenant Admiral Maarten Harpertszoom Tromp, the greatest sea commander of the age, to be ready to sail to protect Dutch merchantmen from search. What actually followed was a matter of dispute between the Dutch and English accounts, each side claiming that it was the other that was guilty of aggression. When Tromp put to sea in execution of his orders, he did not do so with the intention of starting a war, but since he had been ordered not to lower his flag on the demand of an English warship, it was entirely probable that a war would ensue.

Meanwhile on 9 May Robert Blake, with his Rear Admiral Nehemiah Bourne, had left the Downs with 20 ships bound for Rye. En route, however, Bourne with nine ships put back into the Downs. Tromp was cruising off Ostend with some 41 ships, when worsening weather persuaded him to cross the Channel and shelter behind the South Foreland. He sent two frigates to Bourne to explain what he was doing and Bourne reported this to Blake. When Tromp anchored off Dover, he failed to dip his flag, although a shot was fired from Dover Castle to call on him to do so. During the night of 18/19 May Blake tacked slowly up Channel towards Dover, where Tromp had rather provocatively been engaged in musket practice before at noon standing over towards the French coast. At about 3:00 p.m. van der Zaanen arrived with news of the incident off Start Point, and incorrectly suggested

Map 2 The Channel.

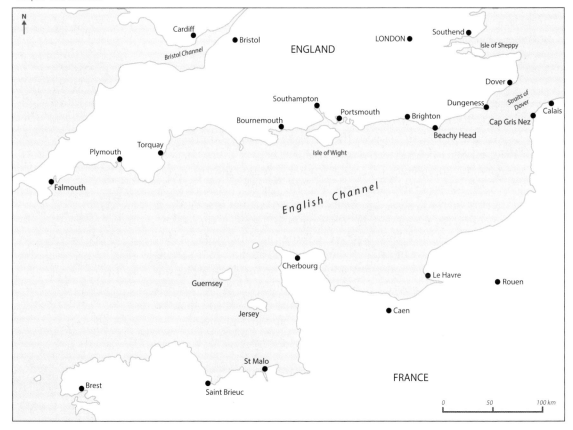

that Blake might have captured the convoy which he had been escorting. Tromp at once set sail towards Blake; the latter had not, in fact, interfered with the convoy, which he found had come from the Mediterranean and would not therefore have goods aboard for France. By 4:30 Tromp was in range of Blake's fleet; signalled by the *James* to strike his flag, Tromp ignored a warning shot but replied with a single shot from his flagship, the *Brederode*. Which flagship then first fired a broadside was hotly disputed; but at any rate the engagement became general and continued until dark. Two Dutch ships were captured, although one was later abandoned and retaken by Tromp's fleet. No English ships were lost, although the *James* was severely damaged.

Reviewing with great care the evidence of who was to blame for the commencement of the action, Gardiner was reluctant to conclude that in their respective accounts either Tromp or Blake was deliberately being untruthful, and suggested that after the Dutch warning shot Blake had fired not a broadside but several shots:

Robert Blake Admiral and General at Sea. A Victorian depiction from 1885. (Rijkssmuseum)

> If Blake followed up his third single shot with the firing of more guns than one, it would be easy for the English to deny and for the Dutch to affirm that he had fired a broadside, and the question would thus be narrowed to a minor inaccuracy. It is difficult to believe that Tromp, having deliberately fired his first gun in such a way as to do no damage, would have fired a broadside immediately afterwards without further provocation.[8]

The engagement, which lasted some two hours, was of course not the real cause of the war, which had by then probably already become inevitable. In a doomed effort to avert it, the States General sent Adriaen Pauw, the Grand Pensionary, to London on 3 June to reinforce the delegation already there. His proposal that the two sides should appoint commissioners to investigate the course of the engagement on 19 May was dismissed by the Council of State as 'dilatory and impracticable.' Confident in their navy, the English felt sure of victory, and on 7 June war was declared.

As has been noted, different considerations had determined the design of the ships comprising the English and Dutch fleets. The largest Dutch vessel, the *Brederode*, which served as Tromp's flagship, was of some 800 tons and carried 56 guns. In the English fleet, however, no less than 14 so-called 'great ships' carried an armament at least equal to or superior to that of the *Brederode*. The largest of these was the *Sovereign*, as she was known in 1652. She was launched as *Sovereign of the Seas* in 1637, and was subsequently known for a while as the *Commonwealth*; she carried originally 102 guns, though by 1652 her armament had been slightly reduced. Another survivor of King Charles I's 'ship money' fleet was the *Resolution* (formerly the *Prince Royal*) which had been adapted to carry as many as 100 guns, though this had by now been reduced to 80 guns. At the time of the outbreak of the First Dutch war, there was not yet in place a system of rating; the great ships were divided into three ranks, first rank being reserved for the *Sovereign* and the second comprising the larger great ships, while the third consisted of those of 500 tons or less. Supporting the great ships was a fleet of frigates; by 1649 the Commonwealth Navy possessed eight of these smaller, faster vessels. A later development of this type, the *Speaker* class, was a two decker carrying an armament similar to that of a great ship; the *Speaker* herself was of 727 tons, and carried 50 guns.

The strategy determined by the Commonwealth government at the outbreak of war was to concentrate on the Dutch merchant fleet and the trade it bore, which was so crucial to the United Provinces, rather than to treat the Dutch fleet as the first objective. The orders sent to Blake, who lay with his fleet in the Downs, were that he should capture the incoming Dutch East Indies convoy, which was expected to enter the North Sea from the north of Scotland. He was also ordered to attack the Dutch fishing fleet operating off the English and Scottish coasts, while a subsidiary target was the Dutch trade in the Baltic. Additionally, another squadron, under Sir George Ayscue, was to protect English merchant vessels in the Channel, and to capture both Dutch and French ships operating there.

---

8   *Ibid.*, pp.175–176.

Accordingly at the end of June Blake sailed north with about 80 ships to execute his orders. Although he had been told to destroy the Dutch fishing fleet, he gave instructions that only the Dutch warships escorting it were to be attacked; on 12 July he captured 12 of these, but allowed the fishing vessels to go free to return home unharmed. His refusal to make war on the defenceless fishermen was notably humane; but it led to his being severely criticised in Parliament. It appears that an unwillingness to make war on non-combatant fishermen was something that Blake shared with his great opponent Maarten Tromp.[9]

Having dealt thus with the Dutch fishing fleet, Blake went on his way northward in search of the East Indies convoy. Meanwhile Tromp had been assembling his fleet, and the objective assigned to him was the destruction of the English fleet. However, by the time that news reached Tromp that Blake had gone north, the winds were northerly, making it unlikely that he could catch the English, so he sailed instead to fall on Ayscue's squadron in the Downs. This squadron consisted of only 16 ships; Tromp had 83. Luckily for Ayscue, the winds turned foul and Tromp, whose orders were to follow Blake if he could, set off to the north. Ayscue took his squadron down Channel to carry out his instructions.

Admiral Maarten Tromp (1598-1653). Captured by English pirates and sold into slavery, Tromp joined the Dutch Navy in 1622. He learned his trade tackling the privateers from the port of Dunkirk. By 1637 he was the effective commander of the Dutch fleet. He is noted for being the first naval officer to use line of battle deployment and tactics. He was killed at the Battle of Scheveningen in 1653. (Engraving on paper by Cornelis van Dalen (II), Rijksmuseum)

---

9   Michael Baumber, *General-at-Sea: Robert Blake and the Seventeenth-Century Revolution in Naval Warfare* (London: J. Murray, 1989), p.132.

Admiral Michiel de Ruyter (1607-76). One of the greatest of the Dutch admirals, de Ruyter was respected by both his own men and his opponents. Having served both as a soldier and in the merchant navy, his greatest achievement is the raid on the Medway. (Mezzotint and engraving by Jan van Somer after painting by Karel Dujardin, Rijksmuseum)

Tromp caught up with Blake off the Shetlands on 25 July, but almost at once both fleets were struck by a violent gale, and were almost completely dispersed. Tromp suffered most: when the gale subsided he had only 34 ships still with him; the rest were scattered, and many wrecked. There was one compensation for the Dutch: as the storm raged the East India men sailed into the midst of Tromp's fleet and could be escorted home safely.

Both Tromp and Blake returned to port to refit. Ayscue had reached Plymouth by 10 August, and was an obvious threat to the inbound silver convoy from Cadiz, as well as the outbound Mediterranean convoy. Michiel de Ruyter was sent into the Channel to protect these convoys and to interfere with English trade, which he did so successfully that Blake was ordered to proceed from the Downs to reinforce Ayscue. This move was too late: reinforced by more ships from Holland, de Ruyter had sailed west. When Ayscue learned of his approach, he put to sea with 40 ships; de Ruyter had 30, as well as a large convoy. A fierce engagement followed, with neither side gaining the upper hand, but at the end of the battle it was Ayscue who withdrew to Plymouth, and the Dutch convoy had been saved. The English had suffered over 600 casualties; Dutch losses were about 100. De Ruyter recorded in his journal that most of his captains had behaved splendidly: 'the most distinguished achievement had been that of Captain Douwe Aukes, a Frisian, who had threatened to put fire to the magazine when his crew lost courage owing to their extremely perilous position.'[10]

Tromp, meanwhile, had been heavily criticised for the disastrous outcome of his cruise to the north. He was unpopular with Dutch republicans, as an avowed monarchist; in the face of the unjustified complaints about his conduct, he resigned his command and was succeeded by Witte de With, a lesser man who was by no means popular in the Dutch fleet. He was chosen as a man who would carry out the instructions of the States General to the letter; these, based on an incorrect assessment of the relative strengths of the two fleets, were to seek out and fight the principal English fleet. De With told the States General: 'I will gladly lead the fleet towards the enemy. Let it be the devil who leads it away from them.'[11]

De With assembled a total of 44 ships, with eight fireships; with the addition of a further 18 ships under de Ruyter, he had a total of 1,900 guns and 7,000 men. De Ruyter, who certainly did not lack courage, urged caution on de With, pointing out that Blake, now joined by Ayscue, commanded 68

---

10 P. Blok, *The Life of Admiral de Ruyter,* transl. G.J. Renier (London: E. Benn, 1933), p.46.
11 *Ibid.,* p.51.

ships that were heavier, better equipped and more strongly manned, with 2,400 guns and 10,000 men. De With rejected de Ruyter's cautious advice; in Blake, he had an opponent equally keen on a confrontation, and a fleet action ensued near the Kentish Knock on 28 September. It resulted in a heavy defeat for the Dutch, who withdrew after serious losses to Goree. They were not, however, downhearted, and put in hand repairs to the damaged ships and collected reinforcements. Most importantly, Tromp was reinstated in command. The strategy now adopted by the States General was an uneasy compromise between offence and defence. Tromp's instructions still displayed a lack of clear understanding on the part of the Dutch statesman:

> It is the first and principal object of the state to do all possible harm to the English with the fleet to be sent out, and for that end a superior body of ships is to be kept together in order that they may put to sea about 22 October to the damage and offence of the English and also to give convoy to the West.[12]

Meanwhile in London the Council of State was also falling into strategical error. News that the squadron under Badiley had been defeated by a stronger Dutch force under van Galen off Monte Cristo, 70 miles south of Leghorn, led to the detachment of 20 of Blake's ships for the Mediterranean. Badiley had taken refuge in Leghorn, and was blockaded there. Blake was not consulted; and the decision was taken in spite of intelligence that the Dutch were busily preparing their fleet for sea. On 24 November Tromp appeared off Margate with 80 ships, as well as a huge convoy of merchantmen. Blake had only 42 ships, but in spite of this on 30 November launched an attack on Tromp's fleet. This took place off Dungeness; the English had the advantage of being to windward, but it was not until 3:00 p.m. that the battle began; the short winter's day meant that there was only a limited time for fighting. Blake's flagship, the *Triumph*, lost her foretopmast; the *Garland* and *Anthony Bonaventure* were both taken by the Dutch, and the *Vanguard* and *Victory* only narrowly escaped the same fate. As night fell, Blake retreated to the Dover roads, and reported next day to the Council of State; he opened his account by saying 'I hope you have hearts prepared to receive evil as well as good from the hand of God.' In his report he did not ascribe his defeat to the overwhelming odds which he had faced; instead, he asserted that there had been 'much baseness of spirit, not among the merchantmen only, but many of the State's ships,' and he asked that there should be an 'impartial and strict examination of the deportment of several commanders, that you may know who are to be confided in and who are not.'[13]

The battle of Dungeness left Tromp for the moment in command of the sea, and he was able to sail off down Channel escorting his huge merchant convoy, capturing many English prizes en route. Meanwhile, in the Mediterranean, the attempt to reinforce Badiley failed; van Galen destroyed the smaller English squadron which was unable to join forces with that in Leghorn, and Badiley, ordered out of harbour by the Grand Duke of Tuscany,

---

12 Gardiner and Atkinson, vol. iii, p.23.

13 *Ibid*, pp.91–92.

A contemporary Dutch parody depicting Cromwell and very likely Admiral Blake cast upon the wheel of fortune being turned by a Dutch sailor and the Dutch Lion. (Rijkssmuseum)

was obliged to quit the Mediterranean altogether and leave the Dutch in control there. Before this, however, Blake had got his revenge over Tromp. Cruising mid-Channel, he was on the lookout for a large Dutch convoy which was being escorted by Tromp homeward bound from the Isle de Ré. Tromp, who had over- estimated the effect of his victory at Dungeness, was amazed to find Blake's fleet standing to the south of him on 18 February. He had to decide whether to carry on to the Scheldt or to stand and fight. He chose the latter course; he could not be sure that the wind would remain favourable for long enough to take him all the way up Channel, and he thought he saw an opportunity to defeat in detail Blake's squadron, which had become scattered. Blake was prepared to take the risk of this, and held on with the ships immediately in company with the *Triumph*. Reporting after the battle to the Council of State, he wrote that 'the Dutch Admirall might probably ... have gone away with his whole fleet and we had not been able to have reached him with our main body, only with a few frigates, our best sailers, which had not been likely to have done very much upon them.'[14]

---

14   Roger Beadon, *Robert Blake* (London: Edward Arnold, 1935), p.177.

The battle raged all day, but gradually the English got the upper hand. It continued next day, as Tromp tried to shield his convoy and withdraw up Channel, and again on 20 February, by now off Beachy Head. Tromp's fleet was running dangerously low on ammunition; the battle raged all day, and it seemed that Tromp might be trapped by the headland of Cap Gris Nez. At dawn on 21 February, however, to Blake's disappointment, Tromp's fleet and his convoy had vanished, working their way around the headland to safety. It had, though, been a striking English victory, Tromp having lost 12 warships and 56 merchantmen.

There followed a pause in operations of some two months. Both sides had a lot of repairs to undertake, and both sides had a serious problem of recruitment. In addition, both suffered from grave deficiencies in stores and equipment. Tromp in particular was profoundly affected by what he regarded as neglect. He wrote to the States General on 25 April:

> I have just this moment received news that Vice Admiral de With is come off the Meuse with the forty weak and crazy ships of which he writes; and I am going thither in person today in the utmost dejection, because a great number of our larger ships have been burnt, sunk and taken, and those that are left remaining we shall be forced to leave lying at home.[15]

He went on to say that, although unwillingly, he would obey the commands of the States General, unless he was granted leave to retire. He had, he said, 'not failed, in season and out of season, in writing and by word-of-mouth, to set forth our danger at sea and the power of the enemy.' His view was that the fleet should not be expected both to fight the enemy and protect the convoys; one thing should be done at a time. The economic necessity of resuming the trade was paramount, so Tromp decided to escort the outward bound convoy northward and then pick up and escort the rich homeward bound convoy as it came around the North of Scotland. With 80 ships, he sailed north on 4 May escorting some 200 merchantmen.

Intelligence reached England at the beginning of May that Tromp was almost ready to sail, and the English fleet under Monck and Deane sailed from the Downs to intercept. On reaching the Dutch coast they found they were too late, and so set off in pursuit of Tromp. He, however, had a good start; he evaded his pursuers, sent on his outbound convoy, and then collected and returned home safely on 20 May with the incoming convoy. Monck, returning from the north, again missed Tromp when the latter put to sea in the hope of catching an isolated English squadron in the Downs; but then, on 1 June, the two fleets met near the Gabbard. Tromp had been reinforced to a total of 100 ships; the English were without Blake, who was with a squadron in the Gunfleet at the mouth of the Thames, but nevertheless they had 105 ships mounting 3,817 guns. The fleet was jointly commanded by Monck and Deane aboard the flagship *Resolution*. The battle was fiercely contested over two days; Deane was killed early in the battle and Monck,

---

15 Gardiner and Atkinson, vol. iv, p.377.

George Monck (1608-70), first Duke of Albemarle. English admiral and statesman, studio of Sir Peter Lely. Monck was to play a pivotal role in the restoration of the Stuart monarchy. The returning Charles II was to bestow many titles and positions upon him for his services, deep in gratitude. By 1664, Monck oversaw the Admiralty, and fought at the Four Days' Battle in 1666. He later fought at the St James' Day Battle. His last action was taking part in the defence of the Medway in 1667. (Oil on canvas, Rijksmuseum)

fearing the demoralising effect, tore off his cloak and covered the body, ordering that it be taken below.

When he realised that he could not force a victory, Tromp drew off towards Ostend as night fell. At daybreak on 2 June, in a dead calm, Monck lay off Ostend in full view of the Dutch. He summoned his flag officers aboard the *Resolution*:

Monck, if still ignorant of naval warfare, knew not merely how to inspire confidence, but when to take advice. The officers were in favour of an immediate engagement, and in order to avoid the faint-heartedness which had been prominent in the early part of the first action, it was agreed that all divisions should attack at the same time and so pierce the enemy's line in three places, if that should be possible.[16]

Monck's boldness was rewarded: at about noon a favourable wind enabled the English to close the enemy, and so furious was their attack that some 70 Dutch ships pulled out of the action. Thus deserted, Tromp could only withdraw; as he fell back to the safety of the entrance to the Scheldt, he left 11 ships in English hands while another seven had been sunk. Witte de With angrily told the States General that the English were now masters of the seas, and this judgment was undeniable.

The economic consequences for the Dutch were disastrous. The fishing fleets were paralysed; merchant ships, laden with exports, remained at anchor, and the blockade which Monck and Blake instituted prevented inbound convoys from returning. A victory at sea was essential if a humiliating peace was to be avoided. This called for a fresh effort to revive the Dutch fleet and, as before, this was achieved to a remarkable extent. One problem was that de With, with part of the fleet, was in the Helder, while Tromp with the remainder was in the Scheldt, and it was essential that they be united; to achieve that in the presence of the enemy was a difficult task. Blake was absent, seriously ill, when Tromp put to sea on 23 July with 81 ships; Monck lay off the Texel, blocking the 25 ships there. Tromp boldly sailed for the Texel, and Monck, who had 130 ships, stood down to meet him. This enabled the Texel detachment to put to sea and join Tromp. On 31 July another savage battle, remarkable for its ferocity, was fought off Scheveningen. It was a smashing victory for the English; they claimed that between 30 and 40 Dutch ships were taken or destroyed, although the Dutch admitted to only 19. Even more catastrophic for the Dutch, however, was the death of Tromp. Struck by a

16   Oliver Warner, *Hero of the Restoration: A Life of General George Monck, 1st Duke of Albemarle, K.G.* (London: Jarrolds, 1936), p.108.

A German newsletter satirising the Dutch and their relations with Cromwell and the King of Sweden, ca. 1657-1658. (Rijkssmuseum)

Oliver Cromwell (1599-1658). A Dutch allegorical cartoon attacking Cromwell. The Lord Protector is depicted tackling a Dutchman and a Spaniard, whilst a Scots and Irish man cower at his feet begging for his mercy. (Engraving from a Dutch news-sheet, Rijksmuseum)

musket ball early in the battle, he was carried below; his last words to his distraught officers were: 'I have run my course. Have good courage.'[17]

Monck, whose fleet had lost only two ships, returned to port to effect repairs. The blockade of the Dutch coast was almost at once resumed, although a substantial number of Dutch merchantmen were able to evade it. Both in England and in the United Provinces there was a careful review of the wisdom of keeping the fleet active during the winter; and both the Council of State and the States General concluded that the wiser course was to spend the winter months refitting for a fresh campaign in the following year.

But there was to be no fresh campaign. In England, the Rump Parliament had been overthrown, and Cromwell had installed himself as Protector. He saw no useful purpose in continuing the war, or insisting on terms so harsh that it could not be ended, and on 5 April 1654, by the Treaty of Westminster,

---

17   Hainsworth and Churches, p.86.

peace was signed. It was possible to achieve peace principally as the result of a secret bargain between Jan de Witt, the newly appointed Grand Pensionary, and Cromwell, whereby neither the infant William III nor any member of the house of Orange should ever again become Stadtholder or Captain and Admiral General. After getting the basic treaty through the States General, de Witt prevailed on the States of Holland to pass an Act of Exclusion to this effect. This, from Cromwell's point of view, removed any threat to republican England from any future Prince of Orange, who would be the only ruler who might provide the Stuarts with a fleet to effect a restoration. Nevertheless it was ominous that the issues which had led to war in the first place remained unresolved. Cromwell's leniency was sharply criticised by those who would have stood to gain by the infliction of greater damage on the Dutch economy, and it was certainly true that the return to the status quo was to the advantage of the Dutch merchants. Dutch shipowners had, however, to bear the losses of some 1,200 merchant vessels taken or sunk during the war. The Dutch had learned the hard way just how vulnerable their precious trade was to English mastery of the seas.

2

From Lowestoft to the Medway

To put it at its simplest, the primary reason for the outbreak of the Second Anglo-Dutch war was commercial greed. It is true that King Charles II was also keen to see the overthrow of the republican system of government in the United Provinces, but this was very much a secondary cause. Professor Jones, in his analysis of the reasons for the war, noted that it was not Charles, or Clarendon his Lord Chancellor, that were the proponents of a violent anti-Dutch policy, 'but an aggressive combination of courtiers, junior politicians, naval officers and city merchants which was associated with, and led by, James, Duke of York.'[1] Charles, indeed, wrote to his sister, the Duchess of Orleans, to record the state of public opinion in England: 'I never saw so great an appetite to war as is in both this town and country,' adding that he was 'almost the only man in my kingdom who does not desire war.'[2]

Professor Jones, examining the elements that finally brought the two countries to war, concluded that it was the court and not the City that was responsible. He pointed out that there were relatively few merchants who were members of Parliament, and that those connected with the East India Company 'were not prominent in calling for action against the Dutch.' The most vocal of those arguing for war were not leading magnates or substantial traders. James, and those around him, on the other hand, had very considerable material reasons for promoting an aggressive policy towards the Dutch, being substantially interested in the Royal African Company, which was in fierce trading competition with the Dutch in West Africa.[3] The profits that were to be made in the region derived especially from the slave trade, expressly referred to in a Royal Charter of 1663 in respect of trade with Guinea. The development of the trade by both the English and Dutch trading companies was accompanied by openly violent aggression by both sides.

---

1   Jones, p.145.
2   Quoted Richmond, p.142.
3   Jones, p.151.

There was a conviction on the part of both English and Dutch mercantile interests that international competition between them was essentially a zero sum game. Captain Cocke, a hemp merchant, a director of the Royal African Company and a Cavalier member of Parliament, speaking to Samuel Pepys, put it thus: 'the trade of the world is too little for us two, therefore one must down.'[4] So far as the English were concerned, there was a settled belief that the Dutch trading policies were directed towards their ruin; and much the same view in reverse was held by the Dutch. The memory of the first Anglo-Dutch war, however, inspired in England a belief that another smashing victory could be achieved, and that 'victory would lead to significant increases in the power and prestige of the monarchy and the wealth of the nation.' If this was the view of the court, it was shared to a great extent by those who would participate in the war. Naval officers had not forgotten the rich haul of Dutch prizes taken during the first war, and looked forward to the promotions and glory that would be associated with the victory that would follow.

Johan de Witt (1625-72), Grand Pensionary of Holland, was a key figure in Dutch politics during the country's 'Golden Age'. A strong liberal thinker, his negligence of the Dutch armed forces and their defeats in the *Rampjaar* or 'Disastrous Year' of 1672 led to his downfall and lynching by a mob in the Hague the same year. Following his death, rioters were alleged to have eaten his remains. (Print by Jacob Houbraken, Rijksmuseum)

A long stride towards a formal outbreak of war was taken in 1663 when the Royal African Company sent Robert Holmes with an expeditionary force to West Africa with the intention of driving the Dutch West Indies Company from the entire coast. It was James, albeit as a director of the company, who gave Holmes his instructions, and he can have been in no doubt of the political effect. Holmes's objective was stated to be 'protecting and promoting the interests of the Royal Company, which is the sole end of the present voyage,' but significantly he was empowered 'to kill, take, sink or destroy such as shall oppose you and to send home such ships as you shall so take.'[5] Sir William Coventry, who as James's secretary produced the first draft of the instructions to Holmes, left little doubt as to the probable outcome of the company's aggression when he referred to the Gold Coast as being 'where it was intended by the company that the game should begin.'

Holmes, as had no doubt been expected by his masters, did a lot more than his bare instructions required. The Dutch had seized the important point of Cape Coast Castle in 1663; Holmes recaptured it, and also took all the Dutch settlements along the coast with the exception of Elmina. He finally returned home in December 1664, by which time news of his depredations had prompted Jan de Witt, the Grand Pensionary, to put in hand countermeasures. Skilfully evading the comprehensive espionage system of Sir George Downing, the English minister at The Hague,

---

4   Quoted Richard Ollard, *Pepys* (Oxford: Oxford University Press, 1984), p.129.
5   Richard Ollard, *Man of War: Sir Robert Holmes and the Restoration Navy* (London: Hodder and Stoughton, 1969), pp.86–87.

Edward Hyde, Earl of Clarendon (1609-74). Lord Chancellor to Charles II, ill-health weakened his position and influence at court, and the raid on the Medway was to be the final blow. He died in exile in 1674. (Engraving by Bernard Picart, Rijkssmuseum)

he sent secret instructions to Michiel de Ruyter, who was at sea with a squadron in the Mediterranean. By October de Ruyter was on the West African coast, where he recaptured one after another all the forts and trading posts taken by Holmes, released captured Dutch shipping, seized English goods in reprisal, and asserted Dutch sovereignty in the region. News of this reached England in December, in time to dispel the euphoria that had been engendered by reports of the success achieved by Holmes and to ensure that his welcome home was somewhat muted.

Diplomatic contacts between the two countries made no progress in resolving the ongoing disputes which might have averted war. In part this was due to comprehensive misjudgements on the part of both de Witt and Sir George Downing. De Witt believed that he must at all costs avoid a policy of appeasement. In thinking that a robust rejection of English demands might successfully be maintained, he assumed that the House of Commons would never trust Charles sufficiently to vote him the necessary resources to conduct a war. In addition, he believed that the Dutch navy was by now strong enough to act as a deterrent against English aggression. On the other hand, Downing was confident that the Dutch, when it came to it, would not be willing to fight a war. He was described by Clarendon as 'a proud and insolent spirit who would add to any imperious command somewhat of the bitterness of his own spirit.' Colbert called him the most quarrelsome diplomat of his time.[6] He loathed the Dutch and advised his government that they would back down:

> The belief that the Dutch would not fight was based on one of those complete misinterpretations of the national character of another people which have so often misled statesmen. Anxious as they were for peace, the Dutch were determined not to give way in matters they regarded as vital. Their fleet was as ready as the English; financially they were stronger. If war came they had every hope of driving the English out of the West Indies for good, and they had full and well justified confidence in the skill and fighting capacity of their seamen and in the material strength of their navy.[7]

6   Hainsworth and Churches, p.101.
7   Richmond, p.144.

There was, therefore, little prospect that war could be averted. For the English, the demands which had been made in the abortive negotiations included compensation for ships taken by the Dutch as far back as 1643, the restoration of Pulo Run in the East Indies from which they had been excluded since 1628 in breach of an arbitration award, and compensation for injuries suffered by English ships in the East Indies and for obstructions to trade in West Africa. Although the Amboyna massacre of 1623 had been acknowledged by reparations provided for by the Treaty of Westminster of 1654, Dutch behaviour in the East Indies remained a source of continuing bitterness. While it is not unreasonable to censure the English for their belligerent avarice, the Dutch were no less to blame for the effect of their mercantile policies. Although they argued vociferously for free ships and free trade in the Narrow Seas, through which their most valuable merchant shipping must pass, they applied a vigorous policy of exclusion in the East Indies that was profoundly resented by English merchants.

War was finally declared on March 14, 1665. Dutch war aims were, as previously, protective and defensive. The later Navigation Act of 1660 was proving a good deal easier to enforce than its predecessors. It applied the restriction that imports be confined to those from the country of origin or carried in English ships only to certain specified commodities, which accounted for about half the total imports of England. Other legislation closed loopholes whereby the controls might be evaded. The effect on Amsterdam and London was considerable; it has been suggested that 'by the second half of the seventeenth century, London may well have overtaken Amsterdam as Europe's largest commercial entrepôt.'[8]

Strategically, nothing had changed since the first war. For the Dutch, it was essential to prevent the English fleet from gaining command of the sea. Whether coming north-east around Scotland or up Channel, the immensely valuable inbound merchant convoys could only be adequately defended by comprehensively defeating the English fleet. By the same token the first objective of the English fleet was to seek out and beat its Dutch opponent. At the start of the war it was known that a great convoy from the Indies was shortly expected, while de Ruyter's squadron was still on its way home. If the Dutch fleet was to put to sea to defend the convoy, as it must, it could be brought to action. The Earl of Sandwich was in no doubt of this: 'Methought the hindering of their trade to come home the best provocation to make the enemy's fleet come out.'[9] But it was of course necessary that the English fleet should be in a position where it could be sure of intercepting the Dutch when they emerged. The commanders of the English fleet met in their first council of war, on 23 April, to decide the strategy to be pursued, in the light of the fact that the Dutch fleet was divided, with about 100 ships in the Texel and 40 in the Wielings.

Opinions were divided. The tough and experienced former republican admiral, Sir John Lawson, argued that the fleet should remain in port at

---

8   Sari R. Hornstein, *The Restoration Navy and English Foreign Trade 1674–1688* (Aldershot: Scolar Press, 1991), p.43.

9   Quoted Richmond, p.147.

Harwich, avoiding the risk of storm damage and remaining fully provisioned, until news came that the Dutch were at sea, 'and then go to them'. Sandwich disagreed, recording in his journal:

> My own advice was that the Duke should sail to their coast with all convenient speed, it being of reputation both at home and abroad; by that means also we might attrap any of their ships that might be coming home by the back of Scotland; the Dutch also might be provoked to come to sea quickly, which was the most desirable thing we could have … Prince Rupert did propose the fleet's riding off Goree at an anchor and sending out parties of ten ships each to the Wielings and also to the Texel to watch their motions.[10]

Edward Montagu, 1st Earl of Sandwich (1625-72), by Sir Peter Lely. Montagu was the youngest colonel in the New Model Army. He fought at the head of his regiment at Naseby, just 19 years of age. He supported the Restoration and served as an Admiral for Charles II. As Ambassador to Portugal, Montagu supported the marriage to Catherine of Braganza. He fought in the Second and Third Anglo-Dutch Wars and was killed at Solebay. (Oil on canvas, Yale Center for British Art, Paul Mellon Fund)

In the event, it was Sandwich's view that prevailed, and the decision was to sail with the entire fleet to a position off the Texel. To prevent the two parts of the Dutch fleet joining, it would have been necessary to remain south of the Texel, but this would allow the incoming Dutch convoy to reach safety. The question then arose as to how close in to the enemy harbour the fleet should go. It was decided to put in an appearance with the entire fleet of 94 ships close inshore, and then to retire and anchor some 15 leagues north north-west of the Texel, where shoal water would permit anchoring so far offshore.[11]

The English navy at the time of the Restoration was an extremely powerful fighting force. Although only two great ships were added to the fleet (the *Royal Oak* and *Royal Katherine*) before the start of the second war, there were also a number of great ships that had been built immediately after the end of the first war. These were the *Naseby* (renamed *Royal Charles*), *Dunbar* (renamed *Henry*), *Richard* (renamed *Royal James*) and *Monck*. By now the system of rating warships was coming into effect. Broadly, the great ships became first or second rates, middling ships and frigates became third or fourth rates, and the smaller vessels fifth or sixth rates.[12] The larger vessels were heavier than the largest Dutch ships, and carried more and heavier guns; they were, however rather less agile than their counterparts. In spite of the lessons of the first war, and the strongly held views of Tromp and others, the Dutch had continued to build warships that were smaller than the English, although rather more stoutly constructed than in the past.

---

10 R.C. Anderson (ed.), *The Journal of Edward Mountagu, First Earl of Sandwich* (London: Navy Records Society, 1929), p.181.

11 Richmond, p.150.

12 Angus Konstam, *Warships of the Anglo-Dutch Wars* (Oxford: Osprey, 2011), p.14.

As it turned out, Lawson's original advice proved to have been justified. After a few days, James became impatient, and proposed that the fleet stand inshore again. However, a strong north wind compelled the fleet once more to stand offshore; on 5 May another council of war was held to consider whether it was feasible for the fleet to get at the Dutch by forcing their way in, but concluded that this was too risky. As a result, the whole fleet made its way back to the Gunfleet to revictual and make any necessary repairs.

In one important particular there were tactical differences in the way in which the next battle would be fought, the English having introduced in 1653 a set of 'Fighting Instructions' which had been subsequently refined. These provided for the first time that the ships of the fleet were 'to endeavour to keep in line with the chief,' which would enable them 'to take the best advantage they can to engage with the enemy.'[13] Adoption of this new tactical concept during the remainder of the first war had brought good results, as the report of a Royalist agent after the battle of the Gabbard showed: 'It is certain that the Dutch in this fight (by the relation and acknowledgement of Tromp's own express sent hither, with whom I spoke) showed very great fear and were in very great confusion, and the English he says fought in excellent order.'[14]

Jacob Baron van Wassenaer Lord of Obdam (1610-65), who was killed at Lowestoft when his flagship, the *Eendracht*, blew up. (Print by Jacob Houbraken, open source)

The Dutch had learned the lessons of the first war, and would themselves adopt the tactic of fighting in line. Meanwhile, there had been extensive tactical discussion among the leaders of the English fleet, as a result of which additional instructions were drafted, one of which made a distinction between attacks from windward and attacks from leeward.

On 1 June the first sighting of the Dutch fleet was made by Captain Lambert aboard the *Happy Return*, and James ordered the fleet to stand out to sea. A north-easterly wind gave the Dutch the weather gauge, but they made no use of it, and it was not until 3 June, with the wind now in the south-west, that battle was finally joined.

On both sides there existed a considerable pool of experience on which to draw for the senior commanders of the fleet and the individual squadrons. James, as Lord High Admiral, commanded the English fleet in person, and led the Red Squadron, with Prince Rupert commanding the White Squadron and Sandwich the Blue Squadron. Each had a subordinate Vice Admiral and Rear Admiral. James, who had Sir William Penn as his Captain of the Fleet, flew his flag in the 80-gun *Royal Charles*, with Lawson as his Vice Admiral and Sir William Berkeley as

---

13 Julian S. Corbett (ed.), *Fighting Instructions 1530–1816* (London: Conway Maritime Press, 1905), p.95.
14 *Ibid.*

his Rear Admiral. Rupert's Vice Admiral was Sir Christopher Myngs, with Robert Sansum as his Rear Admiral. Sandwich's Vice Admiral was Sir George Ayscue, and his Rear Admiral Thomas Teddiman. The fleet was composed of a total of 109 warships, including a number of hired merchantmen, with 28 fireships and smaller craft. It mounted 4,192 guns, and carried a total complement of 21,006 men.[15]

The Dutch fleet was led by the not particularly able Jacob Opdam, Lord of Wassenaar, who flew his flag aboard the *Eendracht*, which mounted 76 guns. The Dutch fleet was divided into seven squadrons, in part because of provincial rivalries, especially between Friesland, Zeeland and Holland. Jan de Witt was particularly anxious that if anything should befall Opdam, Jan Evertsen, a Zeelander, should not succeed to the command. Each squadron also had two other flag officers in addition to its commander. The first, second and fifth squadrons were commanded respectively by Opdam, Evertsen and Cornelis Tromp; the latter was on particularly bad terms with de Witt, sharing the Orangeist sympathies of his late father. De Ruyter was not yet returned from his exploits on the west coast of Africa. The Dutch fleet comprised 103 warships, with 30 smaller vessels including fireships, and mounted a total of 4,869 guns; it carried a total complement of 21,631 men.[16]

Cornelis Tromp (1629-91), son of Admiral Maarten Tromp, served in the First Anglo-Dutch War against the British Commonwealth. During the Second Dutch War he saved the Dutch fleet from disaster at Lowestoft by taking command and allowing the greater part of the fleet to escape. (Print by Lambert Visscher after painting of by Ferdinand Bol, Rijksmuseum)

The battle of Lowestoft began at dawn on 3 June. James wasted no time in launching an attack in good weather, which favoured the use of the heavy guns of the English. However, during the course of the morning the Dutch, with heavier ordnance than previously, were able to give as good as they got as the fleets passed on opposite tacks. Some confusion was caused when Lawson was wounded and the *Royal Oak* drifted to windward. By noon a crucial stage was reached, when Sandwich, who in the *Prince* was engaged with the *Eendracht,* was joined by James in the *Royal Charles*. In the fierce struggle that ensued, involving a large number of ships, the *Eendracht* suddenly blew up, killing Opdam and 400 of his crew. The Dutch fleet was now at sixes and sevens; Kortenaar, who would have been Opdam's successor, had himself been killed, and it was left to Evertsen and Tromp each with a section of the fleet, to extricate it. Evertsen headed for the Maas and Tromp

15   A.W. Tedder, *The Navy of the Restoration* (Cambridge 1916), p.120.
16   *Ibid.*

for the Texel. In spite of a spirited rearguard action, Dutch losses were huge; 17 ships were destroyed or taken, and 6,000 men killed or wounded. The English lost one ship, and had 800 casualties. The victory might have been even more crushing had not, during the night, James's secretary Henry Brouncker, come on deck of the *Royal Charles* with what he claimed was an order from James (who had retired to sleep) to slacken the pursuit of the Dutch as they made for home.

Lawson died of his wound; Sansum was killed; and a number of other prominent captains also died in the battle. Nonetheless, when the news of the victory reached London, the public euphoria was enormous; Samuel Pepys lit a bonfire at his gate and distributed money to the local boys, writing in his diary of 'great news, at last newly come … That we have totally routed the Dutch.' In the United Provinces, on the other hand, there were bitter recriminations. Evertsen narrowly escaped death at the hands of a furious mob; three captains, convicted of cowardice, were shot, and others were disgraced. Since de Ruyter had not yet returned, Cornelis Tromp became commander in chief. In England, a serious row erupted when Holmes, put forward by Rupert as a successor to Sansum, was refused the post by James, who appointed John Harman as Rear Admiral of the White Squadron. Holmes, in a fury, resigned; Pepys, who disliked him, wrote: 'Yet Holmes would do it, like a rash, proud Coxcomb. But he is rich, and hath, it seems, sought an occasion of leaving the service.'[17]

Rather than scatter the fleet to various ports to speed the very considerable work of repairing the many damaged ships, James decided that it was politically desirable to keep the fleet concentrated to emphasise the extent of the victory. Sandwich wrote in his journal:

> It was found considerable to preserve the fame of our victory against all artifices which the separating the fleet would give advantage for, for if our fleet were not seen entire after this battle, though our victory were notorious, yet the cost of it would be aggravated and our loss imagined to be very great, which might be of great importance to the affair between France and Holland, and also among our own people.[18]

The fleet accordingly sailed for the Downs, where the work of repair was put in hand. As Sandwich suggested might be the case, the victory had been striking enough to deter Louis XIV from coming to the aid of the Dutch in accordance with their treaty, giving as his excuse that the Dutch had been the aggressors.

The next question for the English fleet was how to intercept the particularly rich convoy coming home, possibly under de Ruyter's escort, but before this could be answered Charles had to decide on the overall command. Shocked by the high profile casualties, he concluded that James, as heir to the throne, must not be risked in battle. His intention was that Rupert and Sandwich, both of whom had done well in the battle of Lowestoft, should be appointed

---

17   Ollard, *Man of War*, p.137.
18   Anderson, *Mountagu*, p.230.

The Battle of Lowestoft between the English and the Dutch under Wassenaar van Obdam, 1665. (Engraving from a contemporary news-sheet by Willem van de Velde (II), Rijksmuseum)

to the joint command, but Rupert would have none of this, suggesting instead that each should command one half of the fleet. Although Rupert was subsequently persuaded to accept the principle of a joint leadership, Charles decided to appoint Sandwich to the sole command, apparently on the advice of Sir William Coventry.

An alternative strategy to the interception of the East Indies convoy and de Ruyter's squadron was a blockade of the Dutch ports to prevent the re-equipping of the Dutch fleet with naval stores from the Baltic. Maintaining a close blockade was difficult, and could be costly in terms of wear and tear, and it was the incoming convoy that was considered to be the best prize. It was accordingly decided to take up a position off the Texel. No convoy appeared; and in fact de Ruyter, who was running ahead of the East India ships, arrived safely in the Ems with his squadron and a large number of prizes, missing the English fleet by 200 miles.

However, another option now presented itself. A large number of the East Indiamen had taken refuge in Bergen, where there were already many Dutch merchant ships. Sandwich's instructions included a reference to the possibility of attacking these vessels; if he found that he was able to take or destroy a considerable part of the Dutch ships, he was 'not to neglect the opportunity of doing it.' This of course would be a violation of the neutrality of the Kingdom of Denmark, of which Norway was a part. However, this was not a problem. In spite of a treaty between the Dutch and Denmark, which entitled the former to uniquely favoured entrance to the Baltic, King

Frederick III had indicated to Talbot, the English ambassador, that he would not object to an assault on the Dutch ships; in return for this deplorable piece of international double-dealing he was to get one half of the proceeds of the operation. Apart from cupidity, he was apparently influenced by the completeness of the victory at Lowestoft, and had been ready to discuss overtures from Talbot to detach him from his commitments to the Dutch Republic. His regular correspondent at The Hague observed that Frederick's decision showed that 'probity is a bourgeois virtue which kings and princes do not cherish or recognise.'[19]

This disreputable operation miscarried. Sandwich sent a force of 22 ships with two fireships under the command of Sir Thomas Teddiman to Bergen. The latter found on arrival, however, that the Danish governor did not have the instructions to facilitate the operation that had been expected, and he allowed only five English ships into the narrow harbour. The Dutch, meanwhile, took up positions for defence. When negotiations with the governor broke down, Teddiman launched an attack, which was largely unsuccessful, not least because an offshore wind prevented the use of fireships. Obliged to withdraw, Teddiman sailed away having suffered extensive damage and some 400 men killed and wounded, four times the number of Dutch casualties.

At the end of August de Ruyter was sent north to escort the Bergen merchant fleet home. Sandwich put to sea on 28 August to look for the Dutch; both fleets were badly affected by a northerly gale, but on 3 September contact was made with the scattered Dutch ships and during the following week several valuable prizes were taken. Sandwich then broke off the operation, and returned with the prizes; but instead of arranging for the sale of the booty and for the proceeds to go to the Treasury, he allowed his flag officers to help themselves, and took a large share himself. James, who thought that the proceeds should have passed through his own hands, was merely the most prominent of the many who attacked Sandwich for his conduct. So great was the outcry that Charles felt obliged to remove Sandwich as commander-in-chief, and in order to protect him from impeachment dispatched him to Madrid as ambassador there.

When de Ruyter put to sea at the end of August, there had sailed with him not only the Grand Pensionary Jan de Witt, but also two other deputies. De Witt had been largely instrumental in bringing about the recovery of the Dutch fleet after the battle of Lowestoft. Never inclined to personal modesty, he claimed that his presence and that of his two colleagues had been of the greatest value. De Ruyter endorsed this, writing of de Witt's conduct:

> His care and his zeal in the exercise of his difficult function have greatly alleviated my task. His wise counsel in all debates held between him and the commanding officers has always been useful. Nothing was beyond the reach of his intelligence in any direction in which he wished to exercise it, and this applies even to matters of which beforehand he had little or no knowledge.[20]

---

19 Jones, p.161.
20 Blok, p.214.

For his part, de Witt recorded in effusive terms his high opinion of de Ruyter's 'more than common patience,' and the 'good courage and steadfastness' of the admirals.

De Witt and de Ruyter concluded that, since the English fleet was now showing no sign of activity, the Dutch should take the offensive. On 11 October, flying his flag in the 80-gun *Hollandia*, de Ruyter led the whole fleet of 91 ships, heading for Solebay, where part of the English fleet was believed to be anchored. Due to adverse winds, the English ships that were de Ruyter's target were able to escape into the Thames, where a large part of the fleet was laid up in part due to the effects of the Great Plague which had broken out in July. For the rest of October de Ruyter blockaded the coast of south-eastern England but at the beginning of November the bulk of the fleet returned home, leaving 18 or 19 ships under Rear Admiral Sweers to cover returning East Indiamen.

During the winter both sides worked strenuously to prepare their fleets for the 1666 campaign. For the Dutch Republic there had come welcome support when Louis XIV finally honoured the terms of their alliance by declaring war against England on 16 January. In April, the belligerent Bishop of Münster, who had allied himself with England, but whose army had been driven back from Dutch soil by a French force, made peace. A fresh treaty was negotiated between the Dutch and the Kingdom of Denmark. From the Dutch point of view, all these developments were helpful, and de Witt and de Ruyter could plan with some optimism.

On 11 April de Ruyter, aboard his new flagship, the 80-gun *Zeven Provincien*, sailed from Rotterdam to the Texel with four other ships. There, he found that the fleet was by no means complete, but in the following weeks its strength steadily increased. On 16 May the Elector Frederick William of Brandenburg paid a visit to the fleet with his nephew, the 15-year-old Prince William III of Orange, and was enthusiastically welcomed. By 5 June the fleet was complete; 97 warships, with eight yachts and four fireships, mounting 4,600 guns and carrying a complement of over 22,000 men, had been assembled and was ready for sea. It was now divided into three squadrons; the first was led by de Ruyter, with van Nes and de Liefde; the second was commanded by Cornelis Evertsen, with de Vries and Banckert; and the third by Tromp, with Meppel and van der Hulst.[21]

With James having been compulsorily retired, and Sandwich exiled to Madrid, Charles returned to the notion of a joint command of the fleet, and Rupert was persuaded to agree, sharing the leadership with Monck. Whereas in making his plans de Ruyter could do so without regard to what the French fleet might do to support him, prudently reckoning that this was 'too uncertain to judge,' the English were extremely sensitive to the French threat. It was known that the Duc de Beaufort had left Toulon with 30 ships to join another squadron at La Rochelle. It was decided, though it is not known by whom, to divide the fleet, 20 of the best ships sailing down Channel with

---

21   *Ibid.*, pp.226–227.

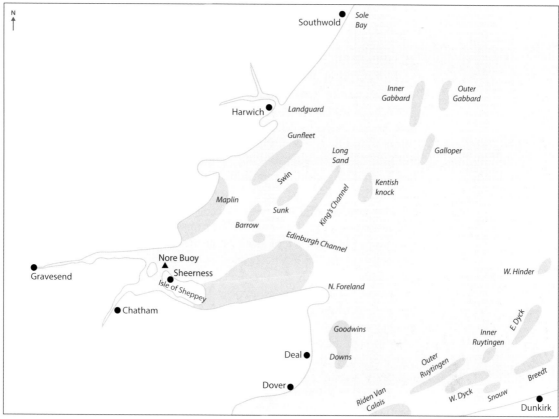

Map 3 The Thames estuary.

Rupert to seek out the French. Later, this very blameworthy decision was the subject of very considerable controversy, no one admitting responsibility.

Thus it was, when de Ruyter came out seeking a fight, and anchored off the North Foreland on 10 June, Monck faced a greatly superior force. He had written strong warnings to Coventry of the disparity in the two fleets, asking for orders as to whether he should fight with the 54 ships he had with him. As Frank L Fox has pointed out in his brilliant study of the battle that was about to take place, Monck was plainly seeking orders not to fight in those circumstances. The reply he got was from James, and it was unhelpful: 'My secretary having also showed me your letter to him in which you desire directions, whether you should fight the Dutch with less than 70 saile I spake also with His Majesty about it, who conceived it best to leave it to your prudence, to doe what you shall think best for his Majesty's service.'[22]

The English had made another mistake, in stationing the fleet in the Downs. This would have been the right location if it had been strong enough to be sure of beating the Dutch, since it covered the Straits of Dover. As it was, it put the fleet into a trap, seriously vulnerable to Dutch fireships, since only to the south was there an exit suitable for a fleet. James advised a move

---

22 Frank L. Fox, *The Four Days' Battle of 1666* (Barnsley: Seaforth Publishing, 2009), p.160.

to the Gunfleet. At a council of war it was agreed to move to the Swin, where the fleet could await the necessary reinforcements. Almost at once, however, news came that the Dutch were out, and orders went to Rupert, who had actually not yet reached Portsmouth, to turn back to rejoin the fleet.

Monck's fleet was organised in the traditional three squadrons; he commanded the Red Squadron, with Jordan and Holmes. Ayscue led the White Squadron, with Berkeley and Harman. The Blue Squadron was to have been commanded by Sir Jeremy Smith, but he was with Rupert; the Vice Admiral and Rear Admiral were, respectively, Teddiman and Utber. There exists some uncertainty as to the actual size of Monck's fleet; he probably had 56 warships with four fireships and 16 ketches. His fleet mounted 3,058 guns and carried 14,335 men. Fox calculates that during the night of 10 June the English fleet was some 17 miles north-east of the North Foreland, and probably about the same distance west by north of the Dutch.[23] In his analysis of the sequence of events after the Dutch were sighted at 7:00 a.m., he notes that the English fleet sailed south-east until getting to windward of the Dutch, when a fresh council of war was convened. Monck had thereby moved to a station from which the Dutch could easily cut off his escape before he consulted his flag officers, and Fox concludes that he had resolved in advance to fight in any case.

Although the odds against Monck made this an unwise decision, he was at first aided by the discovery that the Dutch fleet was still at anchor. Seeking to take advantage of this, he advanced to the attack, taking the Dutch by surprise in the rising wind and lumpy sea. However, the English line became disorganised, and there followed a hard fight of three hours after which Monck tacked to the north west only to run straight into the main body of the Dutch. The fighting continued until petering out at nightfall. Next day the battle was resumed with 40 English ships against 80 Dutch; the odds were overwhelming, and Monck retreated towards the English coast. On 13 June, Monck, after a lengthy calm had been followed by a fresh breeze, continued his retreat and at about 2:00 p.m. Rupert came in sight with his squadron. Fighting began again, but at about 5:00 p.m. Monck's fleet sailed into the Galloper Sand. Several ships grounded briefly, but the *Royal Prince* struck fast, and it was impossible to come to her aid; she was taken, and Ayscue and all but 80 of his crew made prisoner. De Ruyter gave orders that the vessel should be burned. On June 14, with the wind now south-south-west, the English came up with the Dutch, and a further confused engagement ensued before the battle ended in a thick fog. De Ruyter wrote that this had been 'sent by God, who had only wished to punish the enemy for his pride but not to countenance his destruction.'[24] It had been a Dutch victory, though dearly bought with heavy damage to many of their ships. The English lost four ships destroyed and six captured, while a further 30 needed major repairs. Two English admirals, Myngs and Berkeley, had been killed, and one captured. Ten captains were killed outright or died of their wounds. Total casualties

---

23   *Ibid.*, p.190.
24   *Blok*, p.236.

in killed wounded and captured amounted to 4,250 men.[25] The outcome of the battle led to bitter recriminations; Monck blamed some of his captains, claiming that only 20 properly supported him.

The victory was celebrated with extravagant enthusiasm by the Dutch people, though their losses had also been serious. Four ships had been lost, destroyed by fire; total casualties amounted to about 2,850. Three admirals, Cornelius Evertsen the elder, van der Hulst and Stachoner had been killed, with six captains; another captain later died of his wounds.[26]

In spite of the heavy damage to the ships involved, it was not long before the two fleets were again at sea. Monck and Rupert remained as joint commanders with Jordan and Holmes as Vice and Rear Admirals of the Red; Allin, with Teddiman and Utber, led the White Squadron, and Smith the Blue Squadron with Spragge and Kempthorne. The English fleet now comprised 89 ships; the Dutch had 88. De Ruyter was in command; Jan Evertsen came out of retirement to lead the Zeeland squadron, with de Vries and Banckert. De Ruyter's Vice and Rear Admirals of the centre squadron were van Nes and de Liefde, while Tromp led the rear squadron with Meppel and Sweers.

After a spell of bad weather the fleets met on 4 August, St James's day, off Orford Ness. It was another desperately hard battle but this time ended with a decisive English victory. Twenty Dutch ships were burned or captured; the English lost only one. Their total casualties were about 1,000 men, whereas the Dutch lost some 7,000. The victory was followed by the success of a squadron under Holmes, which on 19 August caught a convoy of some 150 merchantmen in Terschelling roads, burning most of them. The flames and smoke of what became known as 'Holmes's Bonfire' could be seen far out to sea. Sir Thomas Allin wrote in his journal: 'We saw divers smokes arise upon the land, which made us judge that Sir Robt Holmes was prosperous, and they continued burning within the night.'[27]

At the end of August de Ruyter put to sea again, with the intention of joining forces with the French Squadron under Beaufort which was heading up Channel to join him, but he was checked by the English fleet and compelled first to take shelter in Boulogne and then to return to his own ports. This left the French in considerable danger, but fortunately for them, the Great Fire of London, which broke out on 12 September, disrupted supplies and Beaufort got away. The Venetian ambassador in Paris remarked that 'the King here

Adriaen Banckert (c. 1620-84), Vice-Admiral of Zeeland. Banckert was a time-served Dutch naval officer, who had first seen action in 1639. Following the Battle of Lowestoft, he was appointed Vice-Admiral. He later went on to play important roles in the four naval battles of the Third Anglo-Dutch War. (Print attributed to J. Dubois, Rijkmuseum)

25 Fox, *Four Days' Battle*, p.273.
26 *Ibid.*, p.275.
27 Ollard, *Man of War*, p.153.

The seizure of the English flagship Royal Charles, captured during the raid on Chatham, June 1667. The *Royal Charles* was used as a floating tourist attraction once captured by the Dutch, and held parties for foreign dignitaries on her. Much to Charles II's annoyance it was broken for scrap in 1673. (Jeronymus van Diest II, oil on canvas, Rijkssmuseum)

recognises the Fire of London as a stroke of good fortune for him. Certainly to it he owes the preservation of his fleet which in its passage through the Channel was only too seriously exposed to destruction.'[28]

There were to be no more fleet actions during the war. This was the result of the misguided decision of King Charles to lay up the fleet on the grounds of economy. In the winter of 1667 what has been called 'the galloping financial deficit of the Navy' was causing profound concern. For the best part of two years the English fleet had fought hard and well, but there was now a growing loss of morale and a lack of belief that the war could be ended as had been originally hoped. Tentative diplomatic feelers had already been put out. In February the King and his Council decided that if the war went on, it would be possible only to send out squadrons of commerce raiders, with the great ships laid up in the Medway. It was a policy roundly condemned by Rupert and Monck; the danger to which it exposed England was sharply illumined when, in the formal negotiations for peace that began at Breda in March 1667 the Dutch took an increasingly intransigent line. De Witt, remarking that it would be 'the best plenipotentiary for peace,' was refitting the Dutch fleet for sea. He planned an ambitious raid on the Thames – so ambitious, that de Ruyter and his admirals were doubtful of the wisdom of risking the fleet in the narrow waters of the Medway and the Thames. De Witt, accordingly, recruited two renegade English pilots familiar with these waters.

---

28 Richmond, p.163.

DIE ACTION VOR CHATTAM VND CHARNESSE.

A Dutch depiction of the capture and towing away of the Royal Charles from Chatham. (Willem van der Stoop, oil on canvas, open source)

He would have liked to accompany the Dutch fleet himself, but could not be spared to do so because of the ongoing negotiations at Breda. Instead, his elder brother Cornelis was appointed as plenipotentiary of the States General with the fleet; again, de Ruyter was prepared to put up with the presence of a political representative, and in fact got on very well with Cornelis de Witt. His brother was particularly concerned to keep the planned assault a secret; and so in part to divert attention he sent a squadron in April under van Gent to harass shipping in the area of the Firth of Forth.

The English could have been under no illusion that the Dutch fleet remained a powerful threat, and was daily being strengthened. In spite of this, the precautions taken to protect the fleet in the Medway were completely inadequate, partly due to incompetence but principally because of the lack of money. Both workmen in the dockyards and seamen aboard those ships that were actually ready for sea were unpaid, and as a result insubordinate and resentful. The soldiers sent to reinforce the crews were of poor quality and in bad condition. The captain of a guard ship lying off Sheerness reported to the Navy Board that hardly any of those sent was worth his keep – they were all 'poor silly lads and raw country fellows.'[29]

De Ruyter sailed from Schooneveld on 4 June; his fleet was scattered by a gale on the following day, when it reached the English coast, and it was not until 7 June that it anchored in the King's Channel in the approaches to the Thames. On that and the following day councils of war were convened to decide how to carry out the attack; it was decided that van Gent with a small

---

29 P.G. Rogers, *The Dutch in the Medway* (London: C. Knight, 1898), p.61.

The Dutch set fire to British ships during the journey to Chatham, June 20, 1667. On the far left is the fort at Sheerness that was taken by the Dutch in the action. (Jan van Leyden, oil on panel, Rijkssmuseum)

squadron should go into the mouth of the Thames, while de Ruyter remained in the King's Channel. On 10 June van Gent took the fort at Sheerness, and next day entered the Medway, where lay the great ships of the English fleet, unmanned and unarmed. After clearing a passage through the ships which had been sunk in the channel, van Gent's fireships on 12 June rammed and broke the protective chain, and he made his way into Gillingham Reach. There he found and seized the *Royal Charles*; Monck, who had rushed to the scene, endeavoured to save some of the other ships by sinking them in low water, but the task was bungled, and Monck was obliged to watch as the Dutch fireships, personally directed by de Ruyter and Cornelis de Witt, approached and burned the *Royal Oak*, *Royal James* and *Loyal London*. Fortunately the *Royal Sovereign* was at Portsmouth; but by the time the Dutch withdrew the operation had cost the English two ships of the first rate, three of the second, three of the third, six of the fourth and one of the fifth rate. The *Royal Charles*, and the *Unity* frigate, were triumphantly towed back to Hellevoetsluis; the great English flagship proved an immense attraction to the thousands of Dutchmen who went to see her. Jan de Witt wrote to his brother in reply to the news: 'God be praised and thanked for such a great mercy; and may He grant that the arrogance of the enemy may be curbed, and the present bloody war changed to an honourable and assured peace.'[30]

For Charles, there was no alternative but to make peace at Breda on the best terms that could be got in all circumstances. Taken overall, in the light of the catastrophic events in the Medway, these were not unduly onerous. Both sides got to keep the conquests they had made, England retaining New

---

30 *Ibid.*, p.116.

York and New Jersey, and the Dutch most of the settlements in West Africa. The Navigation Act was modified to give Dutch merchant shipping greater privileges, and the requirement of the salute at sea was confined to the English Channel. If it meant that the war aims with which England had commenced hostilities had not been achieved, it nonetheless might have been a great deal worse. Pepys wrote miserably in his diary on 29 July:

> Thus in all things, in wisdom, courage, force, knowledge of our own streams, and success, the Dutch have the best of us, and do end the war with victory on their side ... The kingdom never in so troubled a condition in this world as now; nobody pleased with the peace, and yet nobody daring to wish for the continuation of the war, it being plain that nothing do nor can thrive under us.[31]

---

31   *Ibid.*, p.141.

3

At War Again

It was only five years before the English and Dutch were at war with each other again. In that time there had been changes in the shifting pattern of European alliances. During the Second Dutch war the Dutch had had the benefit, for what it was worth, of their alliance with France. In 1668, however, the Triple Alliance between England, Sweden and the Dutch Republic came into being, one of the objectives of which was to bring to an end the war between France and Spain. In the Spanish Netherlands the French had made significant gains, threatening to the security of both the Dutch and the English. Peace in this war was brought about by the Treaty of Aix-la-Chapelle of May 1668, by which Louis XIV handed back the Franche Comté to Spain in exchange for most of the gains which he had made in Belgium.

Louis XIV (1638-1715). Warfare defined the foreign policy of the French king, and his personality defined his approach. Warfare was the principal method by which he could enhance his prestige and that of his country. (Engraving attributed to Philibert Bouttats, Rijkmuseum)

For the time being, therefore, there was a more or less general peace in Europe. In England, Charles was engaged in a continuing struggle to assert his control over government policy in the face of Parliament's desire to make him more accountable. Controlling the government's finances as it did, and perpetually suspicious of the use to which Charles would put the money granted to him, Parliament was a very significant obstacle to his freedom of manoeuvre. He was also obliged carefully to hold the balance between his leading ministers, especially Buckingham and Arlington. Behind all this, Charles was also considering his next moves in foreign policy. Outwardly, he was committed to the Triple Alliance; but his resentment of the Dutch, and in particular the humiliation which they had inflicted on him in the Medway, had not gone away, although plainly now was not the time to do anything about it.

Louis was not unaware of what Charles was feeling and his fundamental aim at this time was to break up the Triple Alliance. In August 1668 Louis sent Charles Colbert, the younger brother of his great minister Jean Baptiste Colbert, to London as ambassador. His primary mission was to explore the possibility of negotiating an Anglo-French alliance. Louis was, at the same time, engaged in negotiations with Jan de Witt, but these were getting nowhere because, confident in the strength of their position, the Dutch felt able to rebuff the French overtures.

In March 1669 Charles took the first step towards a reversal of his foreign policy when he privately put forward to Louis a proposal for an offensive and defensive alliance. One of the conditions of the deal would be for Louis to abandon his naval expansion; and if England went to war, France would support her with ships and troops, and would provide sufficient money to sustain the English war effort. As an added incentive, Charles promised that, for an additional £200,000, he would announce his conversion to Catholicism. Lengthy negotiations followed, partly and most importantly through Charles's sister Henriette-Anne, the Duchess of Orleans. In December, having by now reached the conclusion that another war with the Dutch was inevitable, Charles offered a further deal to Louis. By May of the following year the outline of an agreement had been arrived at, to coincide with the visit of the Duchess of Orleans to England. The treaty, the existence of which was to remain secret, was finally signed at Dover on 1 June.

The fifth clause of the treaty provided that France and England should jointly declare war on the Dutch Republic. The object of this was expressed to be to 'reduce the power of a nation which even has the insolence to aim now at setting itself up as sovereign arbiter and judge of all other potentates.' This was, as Professor Jones observes, 'as clear a premeditated act of aggression as any in history.'[1]

Charles had several motives for undertaking another war against the Dutch, not all of which of course could be publicly acknowledged. One of the principal reasons for tying himself to France had been that Charles saw this as a way to increase the authority of the Crown and to reduce its dependence on Parliament and the militia. The acceptance of a large cash bribe to supplement what he could raise to pay for a fresh war would be an important means of achieving this. The Treaty of Dover also contained several private clauses whereby Charles agreed to suspend the penal laws against nonconformists, including Catholics, and a commitment to announce his own conversion to the Catholic faith at some future date.

Thus while commercial groups no doubt saw a further war successfully prosecuted against the Dutch as offering increased opportunities for the expansion of English trade, on this occasion it was not the City and the merchants who actively set the war in train. There did exist, however, a popular desire for revenge for the humiliation of the Medway, which had come as a fearful psychological shock to the nation as a whole, and to Charles, James and the Navy in particular. This had, in fact, facilitated the

---

1   Jones, p.180.

extraction of the necessary money from Parliament with which to pay for new ships to replace those lost; ironically, Parliament's readiness to vote these funds derived as much as anything else from a very real fear of France and the powerful navy which Colbert was continuing to expand. After 1670, of course, this was not something about which Charles had any such concerns; he was largely indifferent to the wider ambition of Louis XIV to assert his dominance over Europe.

During the peace which followed the Treaty of Breda, neither the English nor Dutch navies had been inactive. During the Second Dutch War, the Barbary pirates had been energetic in preying on merchant shipping, and in 1668 an English squadron was sent to Algiers to persuade the Dey to bring their depredations to an end. Although a treaty was duly signed, the Dey broke it as soon as the squadron left, and in the following year both English and Dutch squadrons were sent to blockade Algiers. For the next three years a vigorous campaign was fought to bring the pirates to heel. In May 1671 Sir Edward Spragge led a particularly successful attack on an Algerian squadron in Bugia Bay; he watched his fireships wreak havoc, and wrote with satisfaction of his 'lovely bonfires, which in my opinion was the most glorious sight that ever I saw, so great a variety in it.'[2] Unfortunately, the peace treaty with the Dey that was negotiated in early 1672 lasted only as long as the peace between the English and the Dutch: once the squadron was withdrawn on the outbreak of war, the piracy was resumed.

The catastrophe in the River Medway had deprived the English navy of all its first rates save one. Only the *Royal Sovereign*, which at the material time was in Portsmouth, survived the end of the second war. The awesome power of the great ships had been conclusively demonstrated during the fierce battles of the war, but they were extremely expensive to build. For King Charles II, perpetually strapped for cash, the task of finding the money to re-equip the navy with ships of the first rate might have been insuperable, but for the rapid expansion of the French navy, which had a profound effect on the attitude of the English Parliament to the need to rebuild the fleet. It was in any case obvious that without a substantial building programme there would be no chance of avenging 1667.

Between 1668 and 1673 the Restoration government succeeded in adding no less than seven first rates to the English fleet. The first of these was the *Charles*, of 1,229 tonnes, armed with 96 guns, launched in March 1668 having been built at the Royal dockyard at Deptford. She was followed in 1669 by the *St Michael*, classified at first, until 1672, as a second rate; she was of 1,101 tons, and carried 90 guns. Next, in 1670, came the *London*, of 1,328 tons and 96 guns; the *St Andrew*, of similar size and armament; and the *Prince*, of 1,403 tons and 100 guns. Finally, there came the largest of these new ships, the *Royal James* of 1671, of 1,416 tons, which also mounted 100 guns, and the *Royal Charles*, not completed until 1673, of broadly similar design, size and armament. New third rates completed in the interwar years were the *Resolution*, *Edgar* and *Swiftsure*, each carrying up to 70 guns, and finally the

---

2   Richmond, p.168.

Harwich, of a similar size and armament but designed on French lines. None of the new ships exceeded the *Royal Sovereign* in size; she was of 1,522 tons, and carried 106 guns. The length of her keel was 127 feet, and her beam was 46'6"; she drew 19'4". The later first rates, though of a lesser tonnage, were slightly longer, and slightly narrower, as a result of which several needed girdling, which increased their beam.[3]

Charles II (1630-85) depicted with his wife, Queen Catherine of Braganza (1638-1705). Upon the Restoration, Charles inherited a history of poor relations with the Dutch created by the implementation of the Navigation Act of 1650. His relations with his first cousin Louis XIV were to cloud his judgement frequently. (Contemporary Dutch engraving on paper)

This major shipbuilding programme was achieved at the expense of lower rated ships; during this period, apart from these larger vessels, only one fourth rate, three fifth rates and four sixth rates were added to the fleet. The system of rating, which at first was somewhat hit and miss, was by the time of the Third Dutch War generally in use, but even so there were still discrepancies between the assessment of ships of the various rates. The system had originally been introduced to standardise the determination of the pay of officers and petty officers, and neither the length of the ship, nor her tonnage, nor her complement or ordnance was decisive. Thus the sometimes entirely subjective classification of individual ships made an accurate reckoning extremely difficult; in 1668 Samuel Pepys, endeavouring to compile a master list of the navy's ships, found that the differences between other lists to which he referred was so great that he was at a loss which to take into account.[4] In his detailed record of the vessels which comprised Charles's battle fleet, Frank Fox provided a comprehensive assessment of the ships with which the Navy fought the Anglo-Dutch wars. He demonstrated the extent to which their fighting power varied, not least in the number and size of their guns. In practice, the difference between the armament of the first and the second rates was steadily disappearing.

Although at the start of the Third Anglo-Dutch war England possessed more of the very largest ships, there was not much difference between the firepower of the English and Dutch fleets. The English began the war with some 27 ships carrying 60 guns or more, and the Dutch with 31. The Dutch, though, had added no new major units to their fleet since the end of the previous war.

---

3   Frank L. Fox, *Great Ships: The Battlefleet of King Charles II* (Greenwich, London: Conway Maritime Press, 1980), pp.95–114.

4   *Ibid.*, p.173.

In preparing for a further war, account was naturally taken on both sides of the lessons that could be learned from what had gone before. The Fighting Instructions which had been issued to English fleet during the Second Dutch War were reissued by James in March 1672 in his capacity of Lord High Admiral. For the most part they followed those issued during the previous war, but they contained three 'Further Instructions.' Julian Corbett observed that these were of the highest importance, and marked a great advance in naval tactics:

> For the first time they introduce rules for engaging when the two fleets get contact on opposite tacks, and establish the much-abused system of stretching the length of the enemy's line and then bearing down together. But it must be noted that this rule only applies to the case where the fleets are approaching on opposite tacks and the enemy is to leeward. There is also a peremptory re-enunciation of the duty of keeping the line and the order enforced by the penalty of death for firing 'over any of our own ships.'[5]

Jean-Baptiste Colbert (1619-83) by Philippe de Champaigne. A very able and energetic politician, Colbert's reform's drove France forward economically. (Oil on canvas, 1655, The Metropolitan Museum of Art, Gift of The Wildenstein Foundation Inc., 1951)

Corbett reckoned that the drafting of the Fighting Instructions marked a return to the belief in formal tactics advocated by James and Sir William Penn, rather than those espoused by Monk and Prince Rupert, whose prescription 'was inclined anarchically to submit all rules to the solvent of hard fighting, and to take tactical risks and unfettered individual initiative to almost any extent rather than miss any chance of overpowering the enemy by a sudden well-timed blow.'[6] Corbett took the view that the more formal principles that were in place hampered the development of fleet tactics until commanders such as Hawke and Nelson 'broke them down'.

For Louis XIV, the possession of a respectable fleet was an important matter of international prestige, but it took second place to his concern to develop the most powerful army in Europe. In Colbert, however, he possessed a minister with the determination to promote France's international trade and to create a navy that would enhance and protect it. He had had to start almost from scratch: the French navy had been allowed to decay, as had the ports and infrastructure necessary to support it. For the harbours and their fortifications he was able to turn to Marshal Vauban, the great military engineer; and for the design and building of the ships that would compose the fleet he recruited a number of talented foreign specialists. In a short space of time Colbert had laid the foundations of a powerful navy.

---

5   Corbett, p.134.
6   *Ibid.*, pp.134–135.

James Duke of York (1633-1701), c. 1665 by Sir Peter Lely, oil on canvas.
Following the Restoration, James was appointed Lord High Admiral. Following the Dutch raid on the Medway in 1667, James oversaw the re-fortification of the southern coast. He was to also command the Royal Navy in the Second Dutch War, fighting at the English victory at Lowestoft in 1665. He was involved in heavy fighting at Solebay in the Third Dutch War, having to transfer his flag to two ships due to heavy damage in the battle. (Royal Collection Trust / © Her Majesty Queen Elizabeth II 2018)

Prince Rupert (1619-82), c. 1670, studio of Sir Peter Lely, oil on canvas.
More than a soldier and a sailor, Rupert was also a patron of the sciences. His mother, Elizabeth of Bohemia, was sister to Charles I, and as such he was cousin to Charles II and James, Duke of York. He commanded squadrons at Lowestoft and in the Four Days' Battle, and the fleet at Schooneveld and the Texel. He also helped organise the defence against the Dutch attack on the Medway. (National Portrait Gallery, London)

Robert Blake (1598-1657), General at Sea, watercolour miniature
by Samuel Cooper.
Recognised as the creator of England's naval supremacy, Blake is certainly one of the most
important naval officers in British history. He is often referred to as the 'Father of the Royal
Navy'. Originally an infantry officer in the New Model Army, he was appointed 'General at Sea'
in 1649. He was to write 'Sailing Instructions and Fighting Instructions' in March 1653. They
are the earliest instructions to be written in any language to adopt the use of the single line-
ahead battle formation. (National Maritime Museum, Greenwich, London, Caird Collection)

Sir Frescheville Holles and Sir Robert Holmes, by Sir Peter Lely, oil on canvas.
Holmes (1622-92), depicted on the right, sailed from Portsmouth with Holles (1642-72) (on the left), to attack a Dutch convoy homeward bound from Smyrna. This action was to precipitate the Third Dutch War. (National Maritime Museum, Greenwich, London. Caird Fund)

Sir Edward Spragge (1629-73), watercolour by Peter Cross.
Spragge, Admiral of the Blue Squadron of the Royal Navy, was a naval officer of Irish descent -
he was drowned whilst fighting his old adversary Cornelis Tromp at the Battle of Texel in 1673.
(National Maritime Museum, Greenwich)

Samuel Pepys (1633-1703), attributed to John Riley, oil on canvas.
Pepys, famous for the diary he kept from 1660 to 1669, was also Chief Secretary to the
Admiralty in the reign of Charles II and James II. This was a post he gained through patronage,
hard work, and a talent for administration. His influence and reforms at the Admiralty were to
have a lasting impact on the development of the Royal Navy. (National Portrait Gallery, London)

Portrait of a Man, probably Sir George Downing (1624-84),
after Thomas Smith, oil on canvas.

The English Ambassador to the States General, Downing was the Scoutmaster General for
the Parliamentary forces in Scotland before coming Teller of the Exchequer in 1657. Shortly
afterwards, he was appointed to The Hague as a diplomat. He retained his post following the
Restoration and set up spy rings that reported directly to him. He was expelled by the Dutch for
his intrigues in 1665. (Harvard Art Museum)

George Legge, 1st Baron Dartmouth (1647-91), after John Riley based on a work of c. 1685-1690, oil on canvas.

Legge's naval career started with the Second Anglo-Dutch War. He was to fight alongside his cousin Admiral Sir Edward Spragge. He fought at Solebay, the battles of Schooneveld, and as Admiral of the Fleet oversaw the evacuation of Tangiers in 1683. (National Portrait Gallery)

While he was developing France's own shipbuilding capability, Colbert arranged for the construction of warships by the Dutch, who built six 74-gun ships for him. By 1668 the French were able to put in hand the building of their own first rates, laying down six of these at Brest and Toulon. The Dutch, however, continued to supply the French with men of war, as Samuel Pepys sardonically observed:

> Between the years '66 and '70 the Dutch built for the French King 10 men of war from 60 to 76 guns, upon the advantage and improvement of their own men of war they built for themselves in the year '65, which they would do for any other prince for money, making shipping a trade rather than a secret.[7]

The ships built by the French were justly very well regarded; so much so in fact that Charles commissioned Sir Anthony Deane, who had carried out a survey of the French *Superbe* in 1672 when the French fleet visited Portsmouth, to build a third rate 'as near as he could of the *Superbe's* dimension.' This was the *Harwich*, referred to above, which was launched in 1674.[8]

National prejudice, however, was so strong that even where there was evidence that a foreign built ship was superior to its English equivalent, commanders preferred the domestic variety, as Pepys remarked:

> And although one country thus gains improvement from another, yet the Dutch, French, Spaniards and English keep generally to their several manners of building and their own country fashion. Nay, such is the humour of the commanders and seamen, that they will incline to go in a far lesser ship of their own built than in a greater foreign built. Witness our commanders loathing a Dutch ship, and the Dutch commanders the same with an English; and so each country the like.[9]

Parliament's willingness to provide funds for the navy amounting to £800,000 had enabled the English shipbuilding programme to continue, and reassured Charles that he could go on reshaping his foreign policy in the way he wanted. His next step was to withdraw from the Triple Alliance, which he justified by a complaint about Dutch pamphlets which contained scurrilous abuse of England, and about the production of medals which he claimed were insulting. Seriously alarmed by the aggressive tone of English communications, the Dutch withdrew the pamphlets and medals that had prompted the complaint and offered to negotiate a new alliance. This offer was, predictably, refused.

Charles still needed to find a convincing *casus belli*. There were few credible pretexts that could be found to justify war, but nevertheless a string of complaints was put together. The most significant of these concerned, once again, the principle of English sovereignty at sea, by which foreign ships must strike their flags in salute to English men-of-war. In support of this an incident was contrived that was intended to dramatise the issue. Charles had

---

7   J.R. Tanner (ed.), *Samuel Pepys's Naval Minutes* (London: Navy Records Society, 1926), p.242.
8   *Ibid*.
9   *Ibid*.

been represented at this time at The Hague by Sir William Temple, who was notoriously sympathetic to the Dutch, and who had worked to preserve the peace. He had alternated in this post with the rebarbative Sir George Downing, whose attitude was directly opposed, and whose hatred of the Dutch was well known. Clearly, for Charles's purposes, Downing was the man to foment the necessary belligerent atmosphere, and he was duly appointed to replace Temple. In August 1671 Lady Temple was returning to England aboard the 6-gun yacht *Merlin*. Her commander, one Captain Crowe, had been given careful instructions about what he should do on encountering the Dutch fleet at sea. He was to insist that the Dutch ships should strike their flags and, if they failed to do so, to open fire. When on 14 August the *Merlin* met the Dutch fleet, which was under the command of de Ruyter, with Willem van Gent as second in command, the Dutch did not strike their flags, and Crowe duly opened fire. Van Gent, who knew Lady Temple well, came aboard the *Merlin* to pay his respects to her, and asked Crowe why he had opened fire. Crowe insisted that van Gent should strike his flag and lower his topsails; this threat from the 6-gun yacht was hardly likely to impress the Dutch and van Gent explained that his orders would not permit this. Crowe allowed van Gent to return to his flagship, and feeling that he had done enough, did not open fire again. When he returned to London to report the incident, Charles was furious; deprived of the major international incident for which he had hoped, he promptly had the unfortunate Crowe despatched to the Tower of London; although soon released he was not employed again.[10]

Downing arrived in The Hague in December 1671, with instructions to demand that the Dutch formally acknowledge the right of English sovereignty at sea; that van Gent should be punished for failing to strike his flag to Crowe when requested to do so; that English merchants should have the right to trade in the East Indies; and that compensation be paid for the insults contained in the pamphlets and medals which had been suppressed. Downing was expressly ordered to insist that the acknowledgement of the right of sovereignty should be put in writing; if this was not agreed, he was to repeat the request after two weeks, giving the Dutch a final seven days in which to comply; and thereafter he was to break off relations by returning to England.

Meanwhile, in order to distract public attention, Charles intended simultaneously with the rupture of diplomatic relations to publish a Declaration of Indulgence in respect of all nonconformists, and as it happened this was not ready in time. Downing was therefore ordered to remain at The Hague until this was in place, but he was with good reason afraid that the longer he did so, the greater was the risk to his life, due to the extreme hatred the Dutch people felt for him. When he pointed this out, Charles cheerfully replied that he was prepared to take the risk on Downing's behalf. Downing was not amused, and, announcing that he had been recalled, hastened back to London, where he was promptly sent to the Tower on 7 February, where he remained for several weeks.[11]

---

10 R.C. Anderson (ed.), *Journals and Narratives of the Third Dutch War* (Greenwich, London: Navy Records Society, 1946), p.57.

11 Jones, p.181.

Casting about for further pretexts that he could publish to justify a declaration of war, Charles added to the demands previously put forward by Downing a complaint that a tapestry was on display in Dordrecht celebrating the affair in the Medway, and another complaint that guided tours were being conducted over the *Royal Charles*. Louis, in the justification which he put forward for declaring war, cynically offered even less reason for its outbreak, complaining that he had been insulted and that the Dutch had been arrogant.[12] The way in which these diplomatic proceedings were being conducted by the Allies left the Dutch in no doubt that they were bent on war.

Although, therefore, Jan de Witt was being given ample warning of what lay ahead, not a great deal was actually done. It is true that in the late autumn of 1671 de Ruyter was asked to produce a report on what would be needed to equip the fleet for a campaign in 1672, should this be necessary. He delivered his report at the end of December, and the delegates for naval affairs duly approved it, but nothing was done immediately to implement his recommendations pending the confirmation by the various provinces of their willingness to contribute to the cost.

In his report de Ruyter stated that during the spring of 1672 a minimum of 36 ships carrying over 60 guns each with a complement of 400 men must be equipped. A similar number of ships carrying between 40 and 60 guns and a complement of 250 men would also be required, together with 24 frigates of 20 to 30 guns and 100 men. In addition 24 each of fireships, yachts and snows must be made available. This programme would require the recruitment of an enormous number of men, and de Ruyter argued that this should be put in hand at once.[13] It was not until 4 February 1672 that the States General finally acted, and when they did they reduced the number of the smaller ships to 12. De Ruyter was gravely concerned by the delay, writing on 11 January that there should be greater activity in recruitment, and also urging that there should be higher pay. On 22 February he wrote to de Witt that it was already too late to fit out even the reduced number of ships prescribed by the States General. He did, however, succeed in getting Cornelis de Witt appointed as the plenipotentiary with the fleet.

The overall strategy which the Allies intended to pursue was based on an offensive by land and sea. The French army would invade the Dutch Netherlands across the land frontier, while simultaneously the combined fleets would seek to achieve command of the sea by destroying the Dutch fleet. After this, it was planned to launch a seaborne invasion of the Dutch coast. As had been the case in the past, however, the English were not disposed to wait for the formal declaration of war before taking hostile action. As early as January 1672 the belligerent Sir Robert Holmes proposed that an attack be launched on a large convoy of Dutch merchantmen laden with salt and wine, which had put into the Solent and was lying windbound off Cowes. Holmes was in command of a dozen warships fitting out at Portsmouth, flying his flag in the newly built *St Michael*. Many of the ships lying in the Solent claimed to be Hamburg ships, but Holmes was in no doubt that a lot of these were in fact

---

12 *Ibid.*, p.182.
13 Blok, p.303.

Dutch. There were other Dutch salt convoys homeward bound coming from the west as well, and Holmes was anxious to take advantage of the significant opportunity that presented itself. He wrote to Arlington on 26 January:

> If my intelligence be true they have hardly salt enough in Holland at this time to salt the meat they must use for their fleet this summer, and without meat they cannot come to sea; and if the salt be stopped you may be confident that they will be in great want. They will not be able to fish nor provide for their Garrisons or scarce do anything without it.[14]

Holmes was extremely annoyed that his suggestion prompted no response from the government, and all the salt convoys went on their way. It was not until early March that he was able to proceed to sea with orders to fall on Dutch ships. At sea on 12 March he wrote bitterly to Arlington of the chance that had been missed:

> You have let slip the best opportunity that ever people had to destroy those I think you will make your enemies ... The very day I had his Royal Highness's order a fleet of merchantmen passed through the Channel, which I supposed to be their first fleet from Cadiz, another being still behind. Had your orders come but twenty four hours sooner we could not miss this last fleet.[15]

However, next day there was another opportunity to carry out what in any view was a deplorable act of international banditry, when the homeward bound Dutch Smyrna fleet approached the Isle of Wight. It had an escort to which the English squadron with Holmes was much superior, but Smyrna ships, like East Indiamen, were heavily armed. One of these carried 40 guns, and about 20 of the others mounted between 20 and 30 guns. Of the approximately 70 ships in the convoy, only four were totally unarmed. Holmes formed his squadron in line of battle, led by the 70-gun *Resolution*. With the advantage of the south westerly wind, he launched his attack at about 3:00 p.m. Although the Dutch suffered heavy casualties, they had much the best of the engagement. In particular, both the *Resolution* and the *St Michael* were badly damaged, and also lost many men killed and wounded. No more than six prizes were taken including only one of the Smyrna ships. The operation had been an expensive failure; Holmes and his squadron had received their just deserts.

   Naturally such a setback prompted an inquest into the reasons for the defeat. In looking for a scapegoat, many blamed Sir Edward Spragge, who had also been at sea with a squadron heading up Channel towards the Downs, to which he made his way without joining Holmes. This was wholly unjust; had it been intended that he should do so there was no reason why orders to that effect might not have been given. Holmes had seen Spragge pass by on his way east, but did not attempt to speak with him.[16]

---

14 Quoted in Ollard, *Man of War*, p.173.
15 *Ibid.*, p.175.
16 Anderson, *Third Dutch War*, p.7.

4

Enemy in Sight

Not all those who had been at the helm of the English government and navy at the end of the second war were still in place at the start of the third. George Monck was gone, dying on January 3, 1670 the age of 61. Clarendon, the Lord Chancellor, had fallen from power in 1667. The ministry which succeeded him, the so-called 'cabal' from the first letters of their names, was an ill-assorted group of decidedly mixed ability; Arlington and Buckingham were the most prominent. Sir William Coventry, for so long the Navy's most influential administrator, who had played a key role in Clarendon's downfall, had himself in March 1669 been turned out of the Treasury and the Council, due in part to a violent feud with Buckingham. He continued as a member of Parliament, however, and was a vigorous opponent of the French alliance.

James remained as Lord High Admiral; concern about his exposure to death or injury if he led the fleet at sea had evidently waned, as he was nominated to take command of the combined fleets against the Dutch. At the time that war was formally declared, however, neither the English nor French fleets were ready to commence active operations. Nor, as it happened, was the Dutch fleet. All three had still to complete their manning and fitting out, and the several parts of each were yet to be united. For the Dutch, the proximity of their naval ports to each other did give them some advantage. If they were able to prepare for sea in time, they might strike at the English singly, or by taking up a central position in the Channel, prevent the junction of the Allied fleets.

It was left to James to decide where to concentrate the English fleet. It had been concluded, reasonably enough, that 'it was not advisable to fight with the Dutch before the conjunction of the French squadron if it can be avoided except upon some great and manifest advantage.'[1] The strategy to be adopted had been considered at some length at meetings of the Privy Council on 18 April and 2 May.[2] At the first of these, attended by the King, James, Rupert, Arlington, Shaftesbury and Lauderdale, the meeting was joined by

---

1   Richmond, p.171.
2   Professor J.B. Hattendorf, et al. (eds.), *British Naval Documents 1204–1960* (Aldershot: Scolar Press, 1993), pp.196–198

Holmes and Sandwich. It was considered that if the ships were ready, and the Dutch had not come out, the fleet should assemble in the Downs. At the second meeting, however, it was considered that the Downs was an unsafe rendezvous at which to meet the French. Dungeness was now considered to be preferable to the Downs since it was also less far for the French to come. In the meantime James was engaged in getting his fleet together so that it might leave its exposed position in the Medway before the Dutch launched an attack there.

Once united, the Anglo-French fleet would as usual sail in three squadrons. As commander-in-chief, James flew his flag in the *Prince*, at the head of the Red Squadron; his Vice Admiral was Spragge, in the *London*, and his Rear Admiral was Harman, in the *Royal Charles*. Sandwich, with his flag in the *Royal James*, led the Blue, or rear, Squadron; his Vice Admiral was Jordan in the *Royal Sovereign*, and his Rear Admiral was Kempthorne, aboard the *St Andrew*. It had been agreed with the French that if James should be killed or incapacitated the command would pass to Sandwich.

It seems that Sandwich still carried with him the memory of the events of 1665, and their effect on his public reputation. To his friend John Evelyn, when bidding farewell to him before leaving to join the fleet, he remarked: 'I must do I know not what, to save my reputation.' He approached the coming campaign in a profoundly mournful spirit. Many years later in 1694, in conversation at dinner with Samuel Pepys, the second Earl of Clarendon recorded a conversation with Sandwich before he sailed:

> His Lordship then walking with his hands one upon the shoulder of Charles Harbord and the other upon Clem Cotterel's (for his greater ease being then grown somewhat goutish and otherwise unwieldy) told the company by way of reflection upon the then management of our sea affairs that though he was then Vice Admiral of England, and Admiral of the Narrow Seas, yet he knew no more of what was to be done that summer then any one of them ... 'This only I know,' he said, 'that I will die and these two boys (meaning Harbord and Cotterel) will die with me.'[3]

The White or van Squadron consisted of the whole French fleet; its commander, flying his flag in the *St Philippe*, was Count Jean d'Estrées, whose seniority in the French navy made him an obvious choice, notwithstanding his lack of experience and any real naval ability. Second in command was the capable, experienced and quarrelsome Abraham Duquesne; his flagship was the *Terrible*. He was extremely jealous of d'Estrées, who in return disliked him intensely. There were two *chefs*

3   Tanner, pp.386–387.

d'escadres, Captain Treillebois de la Rabesnières, in the *Superbe*, and Captain des Ardents in the *Tonnant*.[4]

Because the French were to constitute the White Squadron there were three less English flag officers than usual, which meant that there was no flag appointment for the choleric Holmes, who must have deeply resented the fact that Spragge and Harman, whom he regarded as his greatest rivals, should fly their flags as Vice admiral and Rear Admiral of the Red Squadron respectively. Holmes remained in command of the *St Michael*, which had been hurriedly repaired after its bruising encounter in the Channel with the Dutch Smyrna fleet.

The Dutch fleet would of course be commanded by de Ruyter, with his flag in the 80-gun *Zeven Provincien*; the van, or left-hand squadron, was to be commanded by Adriaan Banckert in the *Walcheren*, while William van Gent led the rear, or right-hand squadron aboard the *Dolfijn*. Other Dutch flag officers included Vice Admirals Cornelis Evertsen the Younger, de Liefde, and Sweers, and Rear Admirals Jan van Nes, Jan den Haen and Jan Matthhyszoon.

As each side made strenuous efforts to prepare for sea, it was plain that once united the Anglo-French fleet would enjoy a considerable numerical superiority. The English fleet consisted of 65 ships, including frigates in this total, plus 22 fireships, as well as a host of smaller craft. It carried 4,092 guns and a total complement of 23,500 men. It was about twice the size of the French fleet, which comprised 33 ships of the line and frigates, with eight fireships. It was accompanied by four store ships. It mounted 1,926 guns and had a total complement of 10,966 men. When de Ruyter put to sea with the Dutch fleet he would have 75 ships, 36 fireships and 22 yachts and other small craft, mounting a total of 4,484 guns and carrying a total crew of 20,738 men.[5]

Urged on by de Ruyter, the States General did all that it could to prepare the Dutch fleet in time for it to be able to strike a blow at the English fleet before it could be joined by the French from Brest, but the cumbersome system of Dutch naval administration made this impossible, particularly because of the delay on the part of the Zeeland Admiralty. Alfred Mahan noted the opportunity that had thereby been lost: 'A blow at the English fleet in its own waters, by a superior force, before its ally arrived, was a correct

Jean d'Estrées (1624-1707). Born into a noble family from Picardy, d'Estrées' initial career was in the army, in which he served under Louis de Bourbon, the Prince of Condé. Persuaded to join the navy by Minister of Finance Colbert, he commanded the French fleet during the Franco-Dutch War and fought alongside the English fleet and saw action at the Battle of Schooneveld and the Battle of Texel. (Engraving by Pollet after Raffet, open source)

---

4   William Clowes, *The Royal Navy: A History From the Earliest Times to the Present* (London: Sampson Low, Martson and Company, 1898), vol. ii, p.300.

5   *Ibid.*, pp.300–302.

military conception; judging from the after-history of this war, it might well have produced a profound effect upon the whole course of the struggle.'[6]

Mahan also detected a possibility that de Ruyter might in any case have entered the war with the deliberate intention of attacking the French only lightly, on the basis that the Dutch 'may have wished not to increase the exasperation of their most dangerous enemy by humiliating his fleet, and so making it less easy to his pride to accept their offers.' There was also, he thought, the practical military consideration that the French being inexperienced, it was 'only necessary to contain them while falling in force upon the English.'[7]

In any case, as it was, it was only on 29 April that de Ruyter was finally ready to put to sea, and even then he had to wait until Banckert, with the Zeeland ships, finally joined him on 2 May. By then the French fleet and sailed from Brest. It arrived at Spithead on 3 May, where it was joined by the bulk of the English fleet two days later.

With both parts of his fleet now in hand, James wasted little time in taking it to sea, heading up Channel. By the morning of 12 May he was abreast of Newhaven, about five miles offshore, and at nightfall he anchored off Beachy Head. Two days later, at Dungeness, he was told that de Ruyter had been at the Galloper Sand on 12 May. The Dutch commander had decided to strike a blow at English shipping in the Downs, and on 14 May he sent van Gent with 12 of his lighter ships into the estuary. Van Gent faced a small English squadron under Captain William Coleman, which had moved out of the Nore with the intention of joining the Allied fleet. Coleman now retreated to Sheerness, exchanging fire with van Gent as he did so. The latter, finding that the defences of Sheerness had been greatly strengthened since 1667, retired to rejoin de Ruyter, who was anchored off the Gunfleet, on 16 May. Coleman cautiously followed.

By that day, the Allied fleet had passed Dover, and on 17 May it headed north. James now convened a council of war. He was according to Sir John Narbrough, the second captain of the *Prince*, 'very earnest to get up to the Dutch fleet.' There was a fine gale blowing south-by-west, and the council decided 'that in case of separation by weather, etc, that Solebay should be the place for rendezvous; if northerly winds parted us, then Portsmouth.'[8]

Admiral Michiel de Ruyter. (Ferdinand Bol, Oil on canvas, 1667, Rijksmuseum)

6   Alfred T. Mahan, *The Influence of Sea Power Upon History* (Boston, Mass.: Little, Brown, and Co, 1894), p.145.
7   *Ibid.*
8   Anderson, *Third Dutch War*, p.88.

However, those attending the council had a lively expectation that the Dutch might be met with on the following day, when they might 'reasonably hope for some greater success than the vain reputation of beating them home.'[9] There was, therefore, a greatly enhanced feeling of anticipation aboard the Allied fleet as it made its way northward. De Ruyter, who seems always to have had prompt intelligence of his enemy's movements, soon became aware of its approach, and left his anchorage and moved further out to sea. This allowed Coleman to slip past him, out of the Thames Estuary. He reached a position south of the Galloper Sand on 18 May, from which he bore north-east of the Allied fleet. His squadron was immediately taken to be the vanguard of the enemy, as Narbrough recorded:

> We absolutely believed they were the Dutch fleet. We stood with them, commands being given to knock down all the standing cabins in the ship and heave the boards into the sea, which was forthwith obeyed, and the ship made clear for a fight. As we came near to them, we perceived them to be the *Gloucester* frigate and the squadron which came out of our river to join with us. We braced our headsails to the mast and stayed for them and spoke with them. The captain said that the Dutch fleet lay about the Galloper and Gabbard Sands. We made sail and stood out our course to look for them.[10]

At about noon on 19 May the fleets at last came in sight of each other. The wind was south-westerly, and the Allied fleet was directly to windward as de Ruyter closed on a south-eastern course. Throughout the afternoon the English and French squadrons manoeuvred ponderously to get into line, and it was not until about 6:00 p.m. that the process was complete. By then it was evident that there was insufficient daylight for any attack to be decisive, and in any case the two fleets were approaching the shoals off Ostend. At about 9:00 p.m. de Ruyter, whose objective was to lure the Allied fleet into the shallow waters, tacked, and James did the same, remaining to windward. Narbrough was closely observing the movements of the Dutch fleet, and noted that the Allied fleet 'kept the nearer them the better to keep them company, to have the opportunity to fight them as soon as the day gave light, which we greatly desired.'[11] At midnight de Ruyter opened fire at long range, evidently to keep the Allies at a distance, and tacked again. During the night the fleets remained no more than a mile apart, but then a thick fog closed down visibility, followed by a west-south-west gale, and touch was lost. It was not until the morning of 20 May that the Dutch fleet was again in sight standing to the north-west. James tacked towards them; seeing this, de Ruyter also tacked, and stood towards the Flemish coast, with the Allied fleet crowding on sail to get up with the Dutch. The weather continued to deteriorate; hoping that it would moderate, the Allies sailed in order of battle about two miles off. The fleets were getting dangerously close to the coast, and as night fell James gave the order to anchor.

---

9   Richmond, p.174.
10 Anderson, *Third Dutch War*, p.89.
11 *Ibid.*, p.91.

Narbrough had been paying close attention to the movements of the French fleet, and evidently did not much like what he saw, recording that 'this time we were up with the Dutch fleet, the French squadron led the van. They are very tedious in bringing up their Division and very careful to keep the weather gage, a good distance from the enemy.'[12]

At dawn on 21 May there was no sign of the Dutch fleet which, not having anchored, had been driven far to leeward. The Allied fleet got under way at about 3:00 a.m. and stood to the north-west; it was decided to head for Solebay, there to take on fresh water and supplies. With a fresh gale at west-by-north, the fleet made good progress, and anchored off Southwold for the night. It was not until 23 May that the fleet stood into Solebay, anchoring in eight and a half fathoms. In 1672 there really was a bay there, which provided a valuable anchorage for a large fleet, but over the following centuries the encroaching waters have long since eroded the two spits of land that formed the bay.

The Allied fleet was strung out along the coast, as it lay at anchor some two miles offshore. Sandwich, with the Blue Squadron, was the most northerly; then came the Red Squadron, which bore west-north-west of Southwold church tower. To the south, the French lay off Dunwich and Aldeburgh. The process of taking on provisions and water was bound to take several days, during which scouts were sent out to give early warning of any approach by the Dutch. At a council of war on 27 May Sandwich was reported as expressing grave concern that the fleet lay in a position which exposed it to being surprised on a lee shore, but James apparently rejected this view as being overcautious, a suggestion which Sandwich found deeply insulting. Narbrough, however, had on 26 May cheerfully written in his journal that he expected that the enemy would be with them in the morning, if the wind hung easterly.[13]

One man, at any rate, who appears to have been quite unconcerned about the chance that the Dutch might put in an appearance, was Sir John Cox, the *Prince's* flag captain. It appears to have been he who persuaded James that there was no immediate danger. On the evening of 27 May he ordered Narbrough to have the ship careened and scrubbed at daybreak next day, if there was little wind. At 2:00 a.m. in calm weather Narbrough gave orders for the ship to be heeled, and the process of shifting the ballast to tilt her got under way. Such wind as there was, was east-south-east.

At about 3:30 a.m. on 28 May signal guns were heard to the east, and it was seen that one of the scouts, the French frigate *Eole*, was hastening towards the Allied fleet, signalling for the enemy in sight. Soon after this, there could be seen on the horizon the topsails of the Dutch fleet. De Ruyter, well informed as ever as to the situation of his adversary, had seized his chance to make a surprise attack.

The decision to do so followed a considerable debate as to the strategy to be pursued. Jan de Witt and the naval delegates at The Hague had wished for the Dutch fleet to avoid battle, and for de Ruyter to take up a position near

---

12 *Ibid.*, p.92.
13 *Ibid.*, p.95.

the Dogger Bank from which to protect returning merchant fleets; only if a seaborne invasion of the Dutch coast appeared to be imminent should battle be risked. To this, Cornelis de Witt, reflecting the views of the senior officers with the fleet, replied sharply that there was no good position in the North Sea that could be occupied; the only alternative was for the fleet to return to port. Neither de Ruyter nor any of his admirals favoured such a course, and it was decided to give battle close to the English coast if there appeared a suitable opportunity; on 28 May such an opportunity arose.[14]

Sea battles in the seventeenth century were extremely confused affairs, even after the adoption of the line of battle as the basic tactic, and a completely reliable account of the events of 28 May is not easy to put together. Reports by participants were not always consistent, and with the exception of Narbrough's journal offer a very incomplete picture of what took place. In particular, the sequence of events, and the time at which they occurred, is difficult to state with confidence. What is clear, however, is that de Ruyter had achieved just the surprise which he had wanted, and which Sandwich had foreseen, catching the Allies in substantial disarray. To maximise the effect of the surprise, de Ruyter took six ships and six fireships from each of his three squadrons, and launched them in line abreast ahead of his main fleet. This force he placed under the command of Jan van Brakel.[15]

Such a concentrated use of fireships in a fleet action had never been previously attempted. It was de Ruyter's intention on this occasion to employ them as the spearhead of the fleet in order to take the maximum advantage of catching the Allied fleet at anchor. It was a potent threat. Fire at sea has always been a terrifying hazard, and sails, rigging and wooden hulls, and the stocks of gunpowder which they carried, made the warships of the time fearfully vulnerable to the attack of small vessels laden with combustible materials coming alongside and grappling with them. In a successful attack the wooden warship could be set ablaze in a matter of minutes.

The origins of the fireship went back a long way. The use of fire as a weapon at sea began in ancient times, and various methods were used in an attempt to set fire to enemy ships, including the invention of 'Greek Fire' by the Byzantines. Fireships were employed on a number of occasions during the Middle Ages; Leonardo da Vinci gave thought to the question, suggesting the use of a fire raft to destroy enemy ships in harbour.[16] In more recent times fireships had been used by the Dutch in 1584 to destroy the bridge built by the Spanish to block the Scheldt and cut off the besieged city of Antwerp. They were again a key weapon when employed by the English against the Spanish Armada as it lay off Calais in August 1588. Thereafter, in the early part of the seventeenth century, fireships became an essential component of the battle fleets of European navies. In his comprehensive survey of the English navy between 1649 and 1669, J.D. Davies quotes one commentator with the English fleet in 1666 as observing of fireships that they were so important a part of the fleet that 'as without meat there is no living, so without fireships

---

14 Blok, p.308.
15 Hainsworth and Churches, p.174.
16 Peter Kirsch, *Fireship* (Barnsley: Seaforth Publishing, 2009), p.13.

there is now no naval fighting.'[17] Peter Kirsch, in his detailed history of the use of fireships, called them 'the terror weapon of the age of sail.' To many, their use was decidedly unchivalrous, but they were nonetheless regarded as necessary. Kirsch, analysing their use by the Dutch during the Anglo-Dutch Wars, concluded that by the time of the third war, the English had developed tactics to resist them which may have somewhat reduced their effectiveness.[18] Fireships, though, remained a weapon of frightful potential, as the events of the coming battle were to demonstrate.

With the Dutch fleet in sight, there was clearly not a moment to lose. Many of the ships of the Allied fleet were still completing their provisioning, while numerous crewmen were ashore in the Southwold pubs, and the drums beat urgently for their recall. Aboard the *Prince*, Narbrough took immediate action:

> As soon as I received the alarm and perceived that they were the Dutch fleet, I commanded the seamen off the yards, and the ship to be righted and made clear, and the foretopsail to be loosed, and a gun to be fired. I immediately went and acquainted Sir John Cox that the Dutch fleet was in sight, standing in with the wind at ESE. He commanded we should get our anchor aboard, which was performed.[19]

That done, he went below to report to James the imminent arrival of the Dutch. Hastening on deck, James ordered the whole fleet to make sail, and by 5:30 a.m. the *Prince* was underway. To the north the Blue Squadron was the first to get away, and stood towards the oncoming Dutch. As they approached, the breeze slackened, giving the Allied fleet more time to prepare. As it was, though, many of the fireships and smaller craft, anchored close inshore, were effectively becalmed.

The *Royal James* was to windward of most of the rest of the Blue Squadron. Sandwich's flag captain, Richard Haddock, recorded that the squadron had got into line 'as well as the short time we had would permit,' and it was soon engaged with the enemy:

> The Dutch squadron, van Gent Admiral, attacked us in the body and rear very smartly; let our van go ahead without engaging them some considerable time as far as I could perceive. We engaged above an hour very smartly; when the Dutch found they could do no good on us with their men of war, they attacked us with two fireships, the first of which we fired with our shot; the second we disabled by shooting down his yards.[20]

Sandwich had put to sea on the starboard tack, to avoid running into the Red Squadron, and James followed suit soon as he could. Sandwich's forebodings seemed not to have left him. As he left his cabin after putting on full dress

---

17 J.D. Davies, *Pepys's Navy* (Barnsley: Seaforth Publishing, 2008), p.60.
18 Kirsch, p.163.
19 Anderson, *Third Dutch War*, p.95.
20 *Ibid.*, p.166.

The Battle of Solebay, June 7, 1672, just after two o'clock in the afternoon, seen from the northwest. (Drawing attributed to Willem van de Velde, Rijkmuseum)

for the battle, he is said to have remarked to his secretary: 'Now, Val, I must be sacrificed.'[21]

The Blue Squadron should, of course, have been the rearmost, but for the moment the normal order of the fleet was necessarily reversed. To the south, d'Estrées put to sea on the port tack, steering south-east, apparently with the intention of getting into a position from which he could move to take up his correct position in the van. He sent one of his staff to James to ask for orders, but to this James had merely replied 'that he desired he would keep his wind as much as he could.'[22] As a result, d'Estrées' squadron sailed out in a different direction from the rest of the fleet, and for the remainder of the day fought a separate action against Banckert's squadron, which de Ruyter sent to the southward to deal with the French and keep them from rejoining the main fleet. Narbrough observed that 'they fought at a great distance; the Dutch would not come nearer to the French ships, for all that they had the weather gage of the French.'[23] William Clowes, a historian always deeply suspicious of French intentions, hinted that d'Estrées' decision to move to the south-east might have been as a result of orders given to him from Paris, while E.H. Jenkins also suggests as a possible explanation that the French admiral deliberately disobeyed orders from James in taking the opposite tack, rather than misunderstanding them.[24] It is a view that is widely held by historians, though Richmond firmly states that d'Estrées had no alternative but to stand to the southward, because he would not have been able to clear the shoals

21   Richard Ollard, *Cromwell's Earl: A Life of Edward Mountagu, 1st Earl of Sandwich* (London: Harper Collins, 1994), p.257.
22   Anderson, *Third Dutch War*, p.179.
23   *Ibid.*, p.96.
24   Clowes, p.303; E.H. Jenkins, *A History of the French Navy* (London: Macdonald and Jane, 1973), p.50.

had he attempted to take a northerly course.[25] Another explanation was noted by Corbett: he recorded that a French writer early in the eighteenth century observed of the battle of Solebay that 'the French there learned what they did not know before, how to set a great fleet in battle order. I know this particular from one of the first, most senior and most skilful officers we have in the navy.'[26]

In the course of the subsequent engagement between Banckert and d'Estrées, which was fought for some hours on the port tack, their two squadrons remained at long range. According to Dutch accounts, this was because the French bore away to leeward continually, and that Banckert did all he could to get to close quarters. The French, on the other hand, contended that it was the Dutch who insisted on keeping at a reasonable distance. The leading French division under Duquesne 'failed to point up as high as the rest', but as Anderson pointed out, even without that division of his squadron, d'Estrées had 20 ships in his battle line, while Banckert had 21. His conclusion, though, is that the failure to close must have been mainly the fault of the Dutch, since the French could not have steered more than about eight points from the wind, with the shoreline being so close.[27]

Nevertheless, although their action was fought at arm's length, the two sides sustained considerable damage, and heavy casualties:

> This part of the battle was by no means the mere skirmish which many writers have called it. The French flagship *St Philippe* had 67 killed and wounded, the *Tonnant*, her next ahead, had her captain seriously wounded, and so did another ship in this division; while des Rabesnières, who commanded the rear division, was mortally wounded, and his ship, the *Superbe*, badly damaged.[28]

It appears that the total French casualties may have amounted to as many as 450 men. The Dutch, too, suffered considerably. The *Groeningen*, which had been engaged with the *Superbe*, had 52 men killed and wounded, and Banckert's own flagship the *Walcheren* suffered considerably.

---

25 Richmond, p.175.
26 Quoted Corbett, p.22.
27 Anderson, *Third Dutch War*, pp.16–17.
28 *Ibid.*, p.17.

5

The Battle of Solebay

By 7:00 a.m. the two rearmost divisions of the Blue Squadron were heavily engaged; the *Royal James* in particular was in the thick of it. Van Gent's squadron, having allowed Jordan's division to head northwards unhindered, was as has been seen able to concentrate on the centre of the Blue Squadron. Sandwich sent his barge to Jordan with a message ordering him to tack, and to weather van Gent so as to be able to come to the assistance of the centre. This, Jordan, who had been watching the fierce struggle in which both the *Royal James* and the *Prince* were engaged, was already attempting to do. Meanwhile, however, Sandwich's flagship was in serious trouble: van Brakel, in the 62-gun *Groot Hollandia*, had thrust his ship under the bowsprit of the *Royal James*:

> There he lay raking her from stem to stern almost with impunity. This was done half an hour after the action began. In vain Sandwich tried to get free. The floodtide was jamming the Dutchman hard under his bows and nothing could be done without cutting away his own bowsprit.[1]

As the battle wore on, van Gent himself came up in the *Dolfijn*, and engaged the *Royal James* broadside to broadside. Sandwich wanted to board the *Groot Hollandia*, but Haddock advised him against this: by now the flagship had already suffered between 250 and 300 casualties, and a boarding party would have to be drawn from her gunners, thereby reducing her rate of fire. This, in turn, would encourage other Dutch ships to attempt to board her, while even if the *Groot Hollandia* was taken, the floodtide would still hold her fast. Sandwich reluctantly accepted this, and pinned his hopes on relief from Jordan's division, which could be seen to have tacked.

This relief did not, however, materialise, as Haddock explained in his report:

---

1   Corbett, p.23.

> Sometime after, Sir Joseph Jordan (our barge having been with him and gave him my Lord's commands) passed by us to windward very unkindly, with how many followers of his division I remember not, and took no notice at all of us; which made me call to mind his sayings to your Royal Highness when he received his commission, that he would stand betwixt your Royal Highness and danger; which I gave my lord account of, and did believe by his acting yourself might be in his view in greater danger than we, which made my lord Sandwich answer me, we must do our best to defend ourselves alone.[2]

Richard Ollard in his biography of Sandwich, has suggested that Haddock's feelings were a good deal stronger than he expressed in his report, and that he privately never forgave Jordan for what he regarded as 'a base betrayal.'[3] Jordan's own account makes no reference directly to the plight of the *Royal James*, recording only the 'hot disputes' between the *Sovereign* and several Dutch flagships. He did, however add that 'in this smoke and hurry we could not well discern what was done to leeward; but sometimes saw the enemy battering at our fleet, and ours at them to leeward.'[4]

Kempthorne, aboard the *St Andrew*, with the rear division of the Blue Squadron, had in the meantime passed the *Royal James*. As he did so, he became aware that the flagship might be in some difficulty, although in the smoke and confusion of the battle he was unable to make out exactly what was happening to the flagship, as he reported:

> As soon as we came near to the *Royal James*, being somewhat to leeward of him, we discovered a ship on board him, supposing it had been one of our own ships, by reason of the great smoke we could not discern the contrary; at which the Boatswain of the *Mary Rose* lying by our side in a pinnace by accident, by reason he could not find his own ship, I commanded him to row on board my Lord of Sandwich, to see what the matter was, and give him his assistance, we standing away with an easy sail.[5]

The *Royal James* could by then have done with rather more assistance than that afforded by a solitary pinnace, but Kempthorne appears not to have considered it necessary to do any more. He continued for the present on his northerly course, and for the next three hours was heavily engaged with a number of Dutch ships. His report gave little or no account of the rest of his division, but it appears that they followed him in line of battle.

The *Royal James* had meanwhile been inflicting considerable damage on the Dutch ships which assailed her. Aboard the *Dolfijn*, van Gent himself had been killed. Haddock was wounded in the foot, but after going below to have his wound dressed, he sent a message to Sandwich suggesting that an anchor be got out astern; with the floodtide having turned, it should then be possible to cut the flagship free from the *Groot Hollandia*. As soon as the

---

2   Anderson, *Third Dutch War*, p.167.
3   Ollard, *Cromwell's Earl*, p.257.
4   Anderson, *Third Dutch War*, p.171.
5   *Ibid.*, p.174.

anchor was dropped, a boarding party went over to the Dutch ship and seized her, enabling the *Royal James* to be cut loose. That done her boarders were recalled, and she edged to leeward with the intention of making emergency repairs. She was, however, not yet out of danger. Isaac Sweers, with his flag in the *Olifant*, came up with a fireship commanded by Captain van Rijn, famous for having commanded the ship that broke the chain in the Medway in 1667. In spite of all that the gunners of the *Royal James* could do, the fireship came on, and grappled with her. Almost at once the flagship caught fire, and within a matter of minutes she was a mass of flames, burning from end to end. Few of her crew managed to escape the inferno, though one of them was Haddock. Sandwich did not survive; his body, still wearing the ribbon of the Order of the Garter, was found 30 miles away a fortnight later.[6]

Astern of the *Royal James*, the 74-gun *Henry* had also been suffering heavily. She was commanded by Captain Francis Digby, and he had made strenuous efforts to get up to the support of the flagship. She was assailed by a Dutch fireship, from which she only narrowly escaped. Battered by the Dutch ships around her, not only was Digby killed, but so were most of her officers. Another ship which had been endeavouring to assist the *Royal James* had been the *Edgar* which, when the battle commenced, was somewhat to the leeward of the flagship, and was herself seriously damaged in the fighting.

Meanwhile, in the centre of the Red Squadron, the *Prince* was herself in trouble. By 8:00 a.m. she was under fire from seven Dutch ships at close range including the *Zeven Provincien*. De Ruyter had, as was customary, headed for the enemy flagship:

> He merrily pointed to the *Royal Prince*, the Duke of York's flagship, and said to the mate: 'Stuurman Zeger, there's our man,' whereupon the mate lifted his hat and calmly replied: 'Aye, aye, sir, we'll see to it.' Cornelis de Witt, suffering from gout, coolly placed himself in a velvet armchair on the companion of the *Zeven Provincien,* surrounded by his halberdiers in their handsome uniforms in the red and yellow colours of Holland.[7]

There was little wind, the sea being, as Narbrough said, 'as smooth as a milk bowl,' and it was very difficult for the other ships of the Red Squadron to come up to the flagship's aid.

The *Prince* was putting up a fierce defence, however, and no attempt was made to board her. Narbrough described how James 'went fore and after in the ship and cheered up the men to fight, which did encourage them very much.' Soon after 9:00 a.m., just as James ordered that the ship engage the enemy more closely, Cox was killed by a round shot as he stood next to the Duke on the poop; several others there were killed and wounded. Narbrough now took over command of the *Prince*; in his journal he recorded his admiration for James in extravagant terms:

---

6   Ollard, *Cromwell's Earl*, p.262.
7   Blok, p.311.

> I do absolutely believe no Prince upon the whole earth can compare with his Royal Highness in gallant resolution in fighting his enemy, and with so great conduct and knowledge in navigation as never any General understood before him. He is better acquainted in these seas than many Masters which are now in his fleet; he is General, soldier, Pilot, Master, seaman; to say all, he is everything that man can be, and most pleasant when the great shot are thundering about his ears.[8]

By midday the *Prince* was almost totally disabled. Her main topmast had fallen, preventing the use of her mainsail to keep the wind, and her rigging was in ruins. Narbrough ordered two of her boats to take her in tow, in order to bring her head round, in an attempt to join the English ships immediately to the north of her, but it had become apparent that James must seek another flagship from which to command the fleet. Accordingly, he boarded a boat to take him to Holmes's *St Michael*, which had been next astern of the *Prince* in the line of battle. James took with him his chief pilot, Thomson, as well as the Marquis de Blanquefort (a naturalised Frenchman who was close to both James and the King).

In the pall of smoke which hung heavily in the almost windless air, it was difficult for both the English ships around the *St Michael*, as well as the Dutch ships which had been attacking the *Prince*, to see that James had transferred his flag, but it was the Dutch that first spotted this, and they opened a heavy fire on the *St Michael*. She was still heading north-east, and pilot Thomson insisted that she must tack, since otherwise she would run aground on the Red Sand. The *St Michael's* pilot agreed; but almost at once Thomson was killed by a shot that also killed Napier, another officer. The *St Michael* now stood to the southward, and enjoyed a brief respite, since de Ruyter continued to steer north-east for the moment. James sent a pinnace to let the rest of his squadron know that he had shifted his flag. Soon, he was in the thick of it again; his intention now was to try to separate the Dutch fleet into two parts. De Ruyter had by now himself tacked, and both fleets were sailing approximately south-east.

As the *St Michael* came up within cannon shot of the *Royal James*, it could be seen that van Rijn's fireship had laid her on board, and that Sandwich's flagship was ablaze. Realising that nothing could be done for her, James ordered the *Dartmouth* to stand by her to pick up survivors. The *St Michael* was now in the midst of the Dutch fleet:

> We then began to engage again very hotly with the enemy, and cut their line asunder, and parted them, having van Gent's ship with two other flags, and most of his squadron to windward of us, and van Nes with another flag and those with him to leeward of us; Then came up to us Captain Wilshaw in the *Castle* fireship and Captain Legge in the *Fairfax* a little astern of us, who was followed by the Earl of Ossory in the *Victory*, and other ships of our Division and Squadron, who had then found out the Standard, and so we continued fighting with the enemy, having them on both sides within musket shot which made it hot work.[9]

---

8   Anderson, *Third Dutch War*, p.97.
9   *Ibid.*, p.182.

The *St Michael* was being pressed particularly hard by the flagship of van Nes, and James ordered Wilshaw to take his fireship and burn her, but in the smoke he missed his target.

The remorseless battering continued, each side giving as good as it got. The *Resolution* and the *Cambridge*, which had been in company with the *St Michael*, and hence in the thick of the action, had suffered terribly. Sir Frescheville Holles, the captain of the *Cambridge*, had been killed, and both she and the *Resolution* had to bear out of line, their place being taken by the *Victory*, which remained in close company with the *St Michael*. Seeing the *Resolution* bear out of line, Spragge, in the *London* with the van division of the Red Squadron, assumed that her captain had been killed, and sent over Captain Shelley to take command of her. Finding that her captain was well, Shelley returned with the information that the vessel had seven feet of water in her hold.

By now the *St Michael* was herself in a similar condition, with six feet of water in her hold, and her state continued to deteriorate. It was becoming apparent to James that he must again shift his flag:

> We were now so much disabled, and had so much water in hold, that Sir Edward Spragge with some of his division, and other of our ships went on ahead of us, which the Duke seeing, and that the *St Michael* must of necessity bear out of line to stop her leaks and refit, left her, about five, and went on board the *London*, ordering Sir Robert Holmes not to bear away, nor take down the standard till he saw it up in the *London*.[10]

James spent an uncomfortable three quarters of an hour in his boat before he could go on board the *London*, where his standard was hoisted, and the battered *St Michael* then staggered out of line in a sinking condition to make the best of her way to refuge in the Thames. She was followed by the *Victory*, by now so disabled that she too had to bear out of line.

Throughout the day the fighting was intense; one survivor of the *Royal James*, who had been rescued by the *Zeven Provincien*, begged de Ruyter to let him stay on deck, saying that there was 'more done already than in all the Four Days in 1666.'[11] De Ruyter himself had been particularly heavily engaged after the death of van Gent. Although de Witt had sent a message to van Gent's flag captain to continue to fly the Lieutenant Admiral's flag, it appears that the news soon became known to the rest of the ships in his squadron, and according to de Ruyter's biographer caused them greatly to slacken their efforts. This was probably due as much as anything else to confusion resulting from the lack of effective leadership.[12]

Spragge, with the van division of the Red Squadron, had been heavily engaged since about 7:00 a.m. By 9:00 his eight ships were in action with a force of 14 Dutch ships, but he succeeded in beating them off. He claimed in his report that 'one of their great ships sank within musket shot of us.' Several

---

10 *Ibid.* p.183.
11 Hainsworth and Churches, p.177.
12 Blok, p.312.

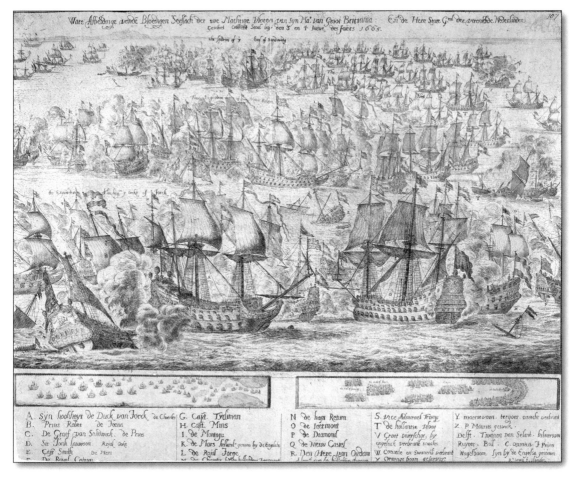

The sea battle at Solebay, between the English fleet under the Duke of York James Stuart and the Dutch fleet under Michiel de Ruyter. (Engraving from a contemporary news-sheet, Rijksmuseum)

of his ships, however, had suffered considerable damage in these exchanges, but when he finally realised that James was aboard the *St Michael*, he ordered the ships of his division to do all they could to get up with the flagship, since they sailed better on a wind than did his own ship, the *London*. The Red Squadron had been joined as recently as 21 May by Sir John Chicheley in the 84-gun *Royal Katherine* which had only just completed her manning. She had been delayed in clearing for action; when she finally joined the line of battle she was engaged with the *Eendracht*, the flagship of van Nes. After a fierce struggle, the *Royal Katherine* was overwhelmed by superior gunnery, and was leaking to the extent that her lower gun ports were underwater; Chicheley had no alternative but to strike his flag, and a prize crew came on board. Chicheley and his officers were taken off the vessel together with about half the crew.

From some way off, Spragge observed that the situation of the *Royal Katherine* seemed peculiar, and he sent Lieutenant Pinn in a boat to board her and find out what was happening. Pinn came back with a remarkable story:

After being in possession of the Dutch three hours the remainder of the crew raised an alarm below that she was sinking. Whereupon the prize crew opened the hatches and called up the prisoners to help at the pumps, but, led by a mild-looking Puritan petty officer, 'a hero,' says Buckingham, 'in the figure of a saint,' they immediately fell upon the Dutch and recaptured the ship.[13]

According to Spragge, they forced some of the prize crew overboard and made the rest prisoners, and intended to take their battered ship into Harwich for repairs.

While he had been out of the battle line, Narbrough had managed to effect some repairs to the *Prince*, including rigging a foresail and mizzen and mizzen topsail, which enabled him to make his way slowly after the two fleets, which were still engaging each other on a south-easterly course. Between 3:00 and 4:00 p.m. he passed what was left of the *Royal James* still burning, with the wreck of van Rijn's fireship stern of her; a number of boats and small vessels were engaged in picking up survivors.

As he pressed on, doing the best he could to make repairs to his rigging as he did so, Narbrough was able to see the *Greenwich*, 60, taking the badly damaged *Stavoren*, which had lost way and was surrounded by English ships. He also saw the *Edgar* finishing off another disabled Dutch ship, the *Josua*, which had been so badly damaged that she had been abandoned.[14]

By mid afternoon a considerable number of English ships had reeled out of line, badly damaged and in a number of cases in serious danger of sinking. Among them was the 80-gun *Henry*, which appears to have had a similar experience to that of the *Royal Katherine*, having been captured and then retaken by the *Plymouth*, with the assistance of the surviving members of her crew. Digby, her captain, had been killed, and she was said to have 'scarce a rope in her' as she made her way slowly back to Harwich. Jordan's division, however, was still to windward of the Dutch as the two fleets continue to head south-eastwards, and was now able some extent to relieve the pressure on the *London* and the rest of Spragge's division.

It was about 6:00 p.m. when Banckert was seen heading back from his engagement with the French, and de Ruyter, signalling to his fleet to form on him, turned diagonally from the wind to meet Banckert's squadron. D'Estrées followed Banckert; after the latter joined the main body of the Dutch fleet and altered course to conform to de Ruyter's movements, the French commander also tacked, to shadow the Dutch as they stood away to the south-east.

Willem Joseph Baron van Gent (1625-72), Vice-Admiral. Van Gent was originally an infantry officer serving in a Walloon regiment. He later raised a regiment of marine infantry, in which he served as colonel. He was soon appointed as a ship's captain and served at the Four Days' battle, St James' Day battle, and helped lead the raid on the Medway in his new position of Admiral. He met his end at the Battle of Solebay. (Attributed to Jan de Baen, oil on canvas, Rijkmuseum)

13 Corbett, pp.24–25.
14 Anderson, *Third Dutch War*, p.99.

The various divisions of the English fleet turned briefly northwards to collect themselves, and then resumed a south-easterly course to follow the Dutch. As darkness fell, they kept de Ruyter's lights in sight until some time before midnight.

By 9:00 p.m. the English fleet had reached a position east-by-north of Aldeburgh, following the Dutch at a distance of some four miles. Of this period, Narbrough wrote:

> We kept on our course SE all this night; a fine air of wind and smooth water. We saw the Dutch lights till 11 o'clock this night; they made more sail than we did and steered a more southerly course, for presently after 11 o'clock I lost sight of their lights. We raised our General's light amain. At 12 o'clock I caused the red flag to be taken down from the fore topmast head and the flagstaff to be struck, for to put up stump vane- stocks and vanes as a private ship, being the General was out of her.[15]

As dawn broke on 29 May the Dutch fleet was out of sight, as was the French squadron. Shortly afterwards, however, the French came into view, and once the whole fleet had been thus reunited, James called for a council of war at 10:00 a.m. The council decided that, having regard to the state of many of the ships, and a marked shortage of ammunition, the fleet should put back to the Thames to refit. Just before noon, though, the Dutch again came in sight, steering towards the Allied fleet from the south-east. The Allies now had the advantage of the wind, the Dutch being to leeward, and James turned towards the enemy, seeking to close. De Ruyter, however had no intention of accepting battle from such a position, and turned back towards his own coast. James followed; during the early afternoon he was almost close enough to engage the Dutch, but at this point there came on a thick fog, which lasted for two hours. The wind now got up to the point that it would have been impossible to use the lower deck guns, and it was decided that no attempt should be made to resume the battle. De Ruyter continued his retirement and the Allies turned back, anchoring for the night near the Galloper Sand, and reaching the Nore on 6 June.

Narbrough, putting the best face on it that he could, thought that the Dutch might have inflicted more damage on the Allies than they did, and claimed 'Glad they are so quit of us, as I perceive by their haste in going away from us.'[16] In truth, though, de Ruyter had won an important strategic victory, having ended the threat of an invasion of the Dutch coast. He had destroyed the *Royal James* and put out of action six of the largest ships in the English fleet, while losing three smaller ships of his own. Anderson calculates that the Dutch lost about 600 men killed and nearly twice as many wounded. The number of Allied casualties is uncertain; Narbrough, not necessarily always a reliable source, gives 737 killed, and as many more wounded, excluding the losses aboard the *Royal James*. A large number of senior officers on both sides had been killed or wounded.[17]

---

15 *Ibid.*, p.100.
16 *Ibid.*, p.101.
17 *Ibid.*, p.21.

Although his bold use of fireships had not brought the stunning success for which he had hoped, due largely to the failing of the wind at the crucial moment of his approach, de Ruyter merited high praise for inflicting such a humiliating reverse on the superior Allied fleet. He entirely deserved the comment of the lieutenant from the *Royal James* previously quoted, who was said to have remarked, in terms not much different from Narbrough's comment on James: 'Is that an Admiral? That is an Admiral, a Captain, a Master, a seaman and a soldier. This man, this hero, is everything at once.'[18]

As events turned out, Solebay was to be the last operation in which James was in supreme command. Reviewing the conduct of the battle, and in particular the relatively limited contribution of the French squadron, Mahan was unsparing in his criticism:

> The truth, which gradually dawns through a mass of conflicting statements, is, that the Duke of York, though a fair seaman and a brave man, was not an able one; that his fleet was not in good order and was thus surprised; that his orders beforehand were not so precise as to make the French admiral technically disobedient in taking the opposite tack from the commander in chief, and so separating the squadrons; and that de Ruyter profited most ably by the surprise which he had himself prepared, and by the further opportunity given him by the ineptness of his enemies.[19]

For de Ruyter, on the other hand, Mahan had nothing but praise, commenting that he showed a degree of skill and vigour which after his time was not matched until the days of Suffren and Nelson.

---

18 *Ibid.*, p.97.
19 Mahan, pp.147–148.

6

Fresh Preparations

News of the outcome of the battle of Solebay was not well received in England, and recriminations began almost at once. Sir Thomas Player wrote in a letter of 4 June that 'people begin to talk discontentedly about the success of the late battle and make horrid reflections on some great people, and I assure you they do not spare the French.'[1] Among the 'great people' who were particularly criticised was Sir Joseph Jordan, for his failure to come to the assistance of Sandwich and the *Royal James*. As for the French, another correspondent wrote of 'the daily graving jealousy against the French,' and the Danish ambassador in London observed that 'this union is not destined to last long.'[2]

Against this background of dissatisfaction, Sandwich's funeral attracted enormous public attention. Charles ordered that he be buried in Westminster Abbey, and on 3 July a procession of state barges came upriver. The funeral barge, draped in black velvet, was followed by the barges of the King, the Queen, James, the Lord Mayor and various city companies. Once landed, the coffin was carried in procession first to Westminster Hall and then to the Abbey, where the service was attended not only by the great and the good, but by a large number of members of the Mountagu family, and by many of Sandwich's retainers and shipmates. Samuel Pepys, grieving for his patron and mentor, carried one of the banners displaying Sandwich's arms, borne beside the coffin and laid over his grave.[3]

The refitting of the fleet was not completed until 27 June, when it left for the Nore. There had been some disagreement as to its proper objective. James, and apparently other flag officers, were all for sailing to the Dutch coast to seek a battle with de Ruyter – if, that is, he would come out. On the other hand, when Charles visited the fleet on 18 June, he brought with him Lord Shaftesbury, who 'persuaded his Majesty that it would be more to his service to endeavour the intercepting of the Dutch East India fleet,'

---

1   Quoted in Richmond, p.176.
2   Hainsworth and Churches, p.178.
3   Ollard, *Cromwell's Earl*, p.262; Claire Tomalin, *Samuel Pepys: The Unequalled Self* (London: Penguin, 2012), p.295.

and this was the operation which James was ordered to undertake. On 30 June, with the fleet some 30 miles east of Lowestoft, James called a council of war at which he announced that the fleet would head for the Dutch coast near Scheveningen and then follow it as far as the Texel before taking up a position 40 miles to the north-east in order to catch the East India fleet. In bad weather, the fleet took up its position, sending out cruisers.

On 10 July, while the fleet was at anchor, another council of war was held. Differing views were expressed. Spragge was emphatically in favour of remaining off the coast and seeking an opportunity to attack de Ruyter. He wrote in his journal:

> I must confess my opinion was to attack first de Ruyter's fleet and then to look out for the East India fleet. The one being a probability sure to be done, the second very uncertain, our fleet being all in a body. The enemy being still 50 capital ships in sea, it was in no way safe to divide our fleet; which, after the enemy were beaten and forced in, might very well have been, so as to find out the Dutch East India fleet.[4]

There were two problems with this, however; one was the direct order to seek the East India fleet, and the second was that it was by no means certain that de Ruyter could be tempted to come out. The decision made, accordingly, was to wait a few more days and then go to the Dogger.

On 24 July the fleet duly moved to the north-east end of the Dogger Bank, and anchored. Next day, however, news was received from the *Cambridge* and the *Bristol* that the Indiamen had been sighted en route towards Heligoland, but none had been taken. The Indiamen went on to reach safety in the Ems, from where de Ruyter fetched them home to the Texel on 10 August.[5]

De Ruyter's fleet, which had been reduced to 47 ships, was seriously undermanned; provisions and munitions had been removed from the ships temporarily paid off, for use on land, and the desperate need to reinforce the army had led to the transfer of a large number of sailors and marines. Although de Ruyter's victory at Solebay had effectively neutralised the superior Allied fleet, and thereby insured that there was no immediate danger of a seaborne invasion, the situation on land was extremely serious. The French campaign there was enjoying almost unbroken success. This was hardly surprising: a biographer of the great French commander Marshal Turenne wrote that 'never had so powerful a French army been opposed to so weak an adversary. So the campaign of 1672 was justly called a military promenade.'[6]

Two armies, one under Condé and one under Turenne, advanced into the Low Countries. On the advice of Turenne, the key fortress of Maastricht was isolated and bypassed, and the bulk of the French forces moved into Holland. Guelderland had been overrun, and Zutphen and Arnhem captured, while Utrecht was under siege. The last city in the path of the French as they

---

4   Anderson, *Third Dutch War*, pp.159–160.
5   *Ibid.*, pp.22–23.
6   General Max Weygand, *Turenne, Marshal of France* (London: Houghton Mifflin Co., 1930), p.194.

Jan de Witt. (Jan de Baen, oil on canvas, Rijksmuseum)

advanced towards Amsterdam was Muiden, and it was here that stood the sluice gates on the River Vecht. While Turenne was held up by the need to occupy the forts along the Yssel, the Dutch took the only step which could stave off disaster by opening the sluice gates to flood the countryside. Nevertheless, the seriousness of the French threat had led to a rising tide of anger among the Dutch populace, focused on the de Witt brothers. On 21 June Jan de Witt was injured in an assassination attempt, and there were mounting calls for the restoration of the Prince of Orange. At the beginning of July, at first in Zeeland and then in Holland, the young Prince William of Orange was formally restored to his position, and the States General appointed him, as stadtholder, to be the Captain and Admiral General of the United Provinces. De Ruyter himself had always had Orangeist sympathies, as did most of those in the fleet:

The official announcement of the elevation of the Prince by the States General, which was conveyed to the fleet by a deputation of the States on July 11 off Westkapelle, made an especially deep impression on the sailors. De Ruyter, who stood outside party strife, noted in his journal that the news 'was very agreeable to hear, to me and to the officers, and to the sailors and to the soldiers.'[7]

De Ruyter, notwithstanding his personal views, had always got on well with the de Witt brothers, whom he greatly respected, and to whom he remained supportive. He was shocked when false accusations were made against them, and when Cornelis de Witt was arrested and tortured on trumped-up charges of attempting to murder the Prince of Orange.

The situation continued to deteriorate, with violent demonstrations, and on 12 August Jan de Witt resigned his position as Grand Pensionary. It was not enough to save him: on 20 August a frenzied mob stormed the prison where he was visiting his brother, and murdered them both amid scenes of appalling savagery. It appears that Cornelis Tromp may have had a hand in fomenting the violent public tumult. De Ruyter's apolitical stance did not save him from the fury of the mob: on 6 September a large crowd surrounded his house where only his wife, her niece and two maids were at home, and it took the courage of a neighbour and the arrival of a company of militia men before the mob could be dispersed.

By now it was clear to de Ruyter that the campaign at sea was effectively over, and he made no more offensive moves with his attenuated fleet. In

---

7   Blok, p.316.

England during early September there were extensive discussions as to what else might be done, and there was some thought of reviving the invasion plan. On 10 September Charles visited the fleet at Sheerness. During his discussions there it was, according to Richmond, the King who vetoed the proposal, while Anderson argues that he was in favour of such an attempt, and that it was the flag officers who opposed it. This does seem the more probable. At all events, it was decided that at that time of year, and without having inflicted a decisive reverse on the Dutch fleet, such an operation would be much too risky.[8] Accordingly, the French fleet was released for the winter and d'Estrées sailed for Brest on 19 September. In the end all that was attempted was to send Spragge with 25 frigates to attack the Dutch fishing fleet. He captured 20 or so of the herring busses, but it was a poor return for the year's campaign, and it was not an achievement that would have impressed Robert Blake, who would have sent them home.[9]

Cornelis Tromp. (Engraving by Michiel Mosijn based on a drawing by Gerbrand van den Eeckhout, Rijksmuseum)

Although after Solebay nothing significant had been achieved by the English fleet, it nevertheless suffered losses greater than would have been caused by a fleet action as a result of the considerable wastage from disease. This was attributable not only to bad vessels, but also to damp, overcrowded and unsanitary conditions aboard ship. Although the beneficial effect of citrus fruits had been known for a century, it seems that these were not supplied to the fleet. By August 23 Narbrough was recording in his journal that he had that afternoon 'set ashore out of the *Prince* 101 men sick, on the King's account, most of them having the scurvy. This day went out of our fleet above a thousand men sick, the major part having the scurvy.'[10]

Charles had sufficient resources to be able to lay up the fleet for the winter of 1672/73; the cost of this, though, and the year's campaign had left him with only about half the money needed to finance a full summer's campaign at sea in 1673. If he was obliged to look to Parliament to obtain the necessary funds, it would be necessary to start the process in November 1672 for these to be raised in time. But if he could avoid doing so it would be greatly preferable, since it was entirely clear that the House of Commons would demand the withdrawal of the Declaration of Indulgence as a condition of voting the money. There was just a chance that Louis might be able to end the

---

8   Richmond, p.179.
9   Hainsworth and Churches, p.179.
10   Anderson, *Third Dutch War*, p.146; Peter Padfield, *Tide of Empires* (London: Routledge & Kegan Paul, 1982), vol. ii, p.91.

war within a few months, and Charles was persuaded by his leading advisers that he should take that chance and postpone the recall of Parliament.

He could not afford to be indifferent to public opinion. One section of this particularly discontented with the effect of the war, consisted of the merchants whose foreign trade had been seriously impaired. This applied especially to shipowners, who were facing heavy losses from Dutch privateers. Although outbound sailings had been resumed after a period of suspension, there were many complaints about delays and about the strength of the naval escorts provided. In the course of this war there had so far not been the compensating factor of any substantial number of Dutch ships taken as prizes.[11]

Convoy work was more or less the only activity on the part of the English fleet during the winter. Narbrough was sent off with a small force to Tangier to arrange escorts for a number of convoys, and then to go to Cadiz to pick up a particularly valuable inbound convoy. He was away for six months, only returning to anchor in the Hope on 5 June. The Dutch, on the other hand, displayed more aggression, sending Jan van Nes with 12 ships and some fireships to attack the large number of colliers that regularly plied their trade down the east coast of England. Thereafter, if possible, his orders were to come back south and proceed down Channel to attack Brest. This venture failed because of foul winds, but it would not, as hoped, have taken the French by surprise, for they had been warned of the planned operation.[12]

William III (1650-1702), Prince of Orange. As arguably one of the pivotal European figures of the late 17th century, William of Orange is perhaps best remembered for having fought France, the dominant power in Europe, to a standstill in three wars. (Attributed to Willem Wissing, oil on canvas, 1680-1710, Rijkmuseum)

The Dutch also planned a much more ambitious mission, sending Cornelis Evertsen the Youngest with three warships and three smaller vessels to raid the island of St Helena, and there to intercept the annual English East Indies fleet. He left on 5 December, but after a clash with an English squadron in the Cape Verde Islands he was obliged to abort the attack on St Helena since the much more powerful English squadron would get there first. Instead, he proceeded to the Dutch colony of Surinam in Guiana, arriving on 15 March. It was to be the start of a very adventurous mission to the Americas.[13]

Back home, William III had been leading the Dutch in a remarkably successful defence against overwhelming odds. He had collected together an army of some 12,000 men, which he stationed at five key strong points commanding the routes through the flooded countryside. He raised a levy of one in every

11 Jones, p.192.
12 Anderson, *Third Dutch War*, p.24.
13 Donald G. Shomette and Robert D. Haslach, *Raid on America* (Columbia, South Carolina: University of South Carolina, 1988), p.83.

two able-bodied men throughout the United Provinces to reinforce his army, and retained for the present the sailors and Marines that had been borrowed from the fleet together with their guns and ammunition. William was a quiet but extremely resolute young man, whose personality was the complete antithesis of his uncle, King Charles II; in his visits to England before the war he had felt extremely uncomfortable in the atmosphere of the lax morality of Charles's court. Sir William Temple described him as 'a most extreme hopeful young Prince … and a young man of more parts than ordinary, and of the better sort; that is not lying in the kind of wit which is neither of use to oneself nor to anybody else, but in good plain sense, with show of application.'[14]

After the end of the campaigning season of 1672 there was naturally much earnest discussion in London as to the correct strategy to pursue in the coming year. On the one hand, the strenuous naval campaign against the trade of the Dutch might have a telling effect on their ability or willingness to continue the war; on the other hand, a seaborne invasion of the Dutch coast might, in conjunction with the operations of the French armies, bring about a speedy victory. In either case, it would be essential first to neutralise de Ruyter's fleet. Characteristically, Rupert was in favour of an all-out assault on the enemy in port. He advocated taking the whole fleet over, forcing his way in, ignoring the navigational difficulties and the threat of the Dutch fireships, and pressing on to attack the Dutch fleet:

> If for some unforeseeable reason it should prove impossible to reach them, if the enemy were able to refuse action and would not fight, Rupert would land an army to destroy the ships from the land. Thus his proposed use of the army was not to invade Holland, but to establish command at sea and open the way for future action.[15]

The alternative strategy considered was to threaten an invasion in the hope that it would compel de Ruyter to put to sea to forestall it.

In the end it was decided to raise an army of 15,000 men, ready to invade when opportunity arose; this would, it was thought, achieve the desired objective of forcing de Ruyter to come out and fight. At the same time an amphibious operation was contemplated. A force of an additional 5,000 men would be embarked on board the Allied fleet to take part in an attack on the Dutch harbours.

At some time during the winter it was decided that Rupert should be in command of the fleet, and that James should direct the Navy from the Admiralty. This was possibly due to the recurring anxiety about the risk of the heir to the throne being killed or injured, or possibly in anticipation of the difficulties that might confront James as a result of Parliamentary action. By early 1673 it had become clear that the gamble on a speedy French victory had been lost; contacts with the Dutch to explore the possibility of ending the war by negotiation came to nothing, and there was now no alternative but

---

14 Padfield, p.93.
15 Richmond, p.180.

to go cap in hand to Parliament to seek the necessary vote for supply. It was calculated that a sum of £1.25m would be required.

The parliamentary session began on 5 February. Secretary of State Henry Coventry (Sir William's younger brother) put the case for the French alliance: 'We have found the dangers of being against the King of France, therefore we joined with him, and he has succeeded beyond expectation.'[16] Charles told Parliament that the war was 'necessary', while Shaftesbury warned of the consequences of not finally crushing the Dutch while they were down: 'If, after this, you suffer them to get up, let this be remembered, the states of Holland are England's eternal enemy both by interest and inclination.'[17] When it came to it, neither the Lords nor Commons opposed the war, and voted sufficient money for the 1673 campaigning season. However, as expected, they made this conditional on the Declaration of Indulgence being withdrawn, and put forward a bill to exclude Catholics from public office. This amounted to a direct challenge to the King, who contemplated dissolving parliament. But Louis made it clear that he would not put up the money that was needed, and Charles was obliged to give way; the Test Act received the Royal Assent on 23 March. This meant that a war that began with the object of increasing the authority of the King had now resulted in a major reduction in his power. In due course the inevitable effect was that James, as a practising Catholic, had no choice but to resign his office as Lord High Admiral, which he did on 15 June.

---

16 Quoted in Jones, p.193.
17 *Ibid.*, p.199.

7

The Two Battles of Schooneveld

In February 1673 Spragge, accompanied by the Earl of Sunderland, was sent off to France to agree the plans for the coming campaign. The talks went well, and on 17 February an agreement was signed providing for both fleets to assemble by 15 April, the English in the Downs and the French in Camaret Bay, after which they should unite at Portsmouth.[1] Rupert seems not to have been consulted about Spragge's mission; if he was offended by this, he was even more put out by the refusal of his request that Holmes should be one of his flag officers. This was on account of the bad relations that existed between Spragge and the combative Holmes. This did nothing for the relationship between Rupert and Spragge; the coolness that existed between them was sharpened, on Spragge's part, by the disappointment that he appears to have felt in not being given the chief command himself, although there was never much likelihood of this.

The instructions given to Rupert embodying the strategy that had been agreed were not finally prepared until 26 April. He was to proceed to Portsmouth, embark all the soldiers and seamen there, and then sail as soon as possible to the Dutch coast, where he was to 'attack any of the States' ships there lying in harbour, or, if you shall find it more for our service, you shall land where you think most proper and there attack what places you shall judge likely to be carried, or destroy and use hostility to the inhabitants and goods as you shall judge most suitable.'[2]

Meanwhile the Dutch had also been considering what their strategy for 1673 should be. They also had a command problem, because William wanted Cornelis Tromp, a passionate Orangeist, recalled to the fleet in the place of van Gent, killed at Solebay. Here again the difficulty was one of personality: Tromp and de Ruyter loathed each other. In March William attempted to bring about a reconciliation, asking them to meet with him. This ended in a violent argument. De Ruyter suspected that Tromp was scheming to replace him. He told William that Tromp was 'a valiant and brave soldier, but not fit to command or to be commanded, he being too furious.' In reply, Tromp was

---

1   Anderson, *Third Dutch War*, pp.26–27.
2   Richmond, pp.180–181.

William III, Prince of Orange and Stadholder. (Caspar Netscher, oil on canvas, 1680-1684, Rijksmuseum)

insulting not only about de Ruyter, whom he said could not fight, but also about his family.

William did not give up, and in April he tried again, calling the two admirals before him, and this time he was more successful. The meeting ended with both men 'promising henceforth to live in brotherly faith and friendship', and on 30 April Tromp was again appointed as Lieutenant Admiral. William, greatly relieved, confirmed in writing to de Ruyter that he had 'commanded Lieutenant Admiral Tromp in earnest terms, to behave towards yourself and your orders with due respect and obedience,' which Tromp had promised him would be the case.[3] Given that Tromp had undoubtedly been involved in the attacks on de Ruyter and his family, the commander-in-chief was showing remarkable tolerance and pragmatism in accepting this.

The immediate plan decided on for the Dutch fleet was that it should sail as soon as possible to the mouth of the Thames, where it was intended to use block ships to prevent Rupert's squadron there from getting to sea to join the French. It was arranged that 11 block ships would sail with the fleet; these would be scuttled in the Middle Ground. By late April, however, only eight block ships were available, and as usual the Zeeland squadron was not ready. De Ruyter could wait no longer, and 29 April he sailed for the Thames. Five of the block ships were to be sunk in the north King's Channel, and three in the south. Arriving off the Thames, de Ruyter sent in a squadron of lighter ships and fireships with what Rupert called the 'sinkers' under the command of Rear Admirals Jan van Nes and Vlugh. With the rest of the fleet he took up a covering position off the Gunfleet. On 2 May the squadron entered the Thames estuary, but the fog was so thick that nothing could be done. The next day was almost as bad, though the squadron did move some way forward; on 4 May the fog cleared, when it was seen that Rupert had been able to emerge and was now lying off the Middle Ground waiting for them. In the face of this, de Ruyter had no option other than to call off the operation, and he returned with the fleet to the Dutch coast.[4]

Rupert reported to the King on 4 May: 'The Holland ships which came to make use of their sinkers are returned to the gross of their fleet in the Sledway.' Since de Ruyter appeared to be in an exposed position before he returned to the Schooneveld, Rupert called a council of war, which resolved to ask the King to direct the squadron at Portsmouth, with or without the

---

3   Blok, p.327.
4   Corbett, p.30.

French, to come up Channel to meet him in the Downs at once; Rupert's plan was that 'if they come thither I shall with our fleet here drive the enemy into a great strait and securely join the French fleet.' It was too late, however, for such an attack, since de Ruyter was safely home again.[5]

The intention was that Rupert's flagship should be the newly completed *Royal Charles*. She was, however, at Portsmouth, under the command of Richard Haddock, whom Rupert had chosen as his flag captain, so for the moment Rupert, on joining the fleet in the Thames, had hoisted his flag in the *St Michael*. Although his opinion of this ship was by no means universally shared, Sir Robert Holmes always maintained that she was a perfect first rate. She was on the small side for the 98 guns with which she was originally armed. The *Royal Charles*, on the other hand, at 1,443 tons, and armed with 100 guns, was a much more imposing vessel. Built by Sir Anthony Deane, she was the sister of the ill-fated Royal *James*, and like her turned out to be an unusually fast ship; unfortunately, as Rupert was in due course to find out, she also had some serious defects.[6]

On 6 May, with the wind in the north-east, Rupert executed a remarkable feat of seamanship. In breach of the standing instructions of Trinity House, he sent forward ketches to mark the shoals. Spragge recorded with admiration in his journal: 'We weighed with all the fleet and turned through the narrow of the Middle Ground with the tide of ebb; never done before by the King's ships.'[7] The fleet then sailed round into the Channel, anchoring to the west of Dungeness on 10 May, to await the arrival of the ships from Portsmouth. These, led by Haddock in the *Royal Charles*, arrived next day, as did a French sloop with news that d'Estrées was by now off the Isle of Wight. The French fleet, hampered by calm weather, finally joined with the English fleet off Rye on 16 May. Charles and James had meanwhile come down with a large retinue to visit the fleet.

On 12 May a Council of War was held on board the *Royal Charles*, to which Rupert had now transferred. The question to be discussed was whether to launch an attack on de Ruyter as he lay within the security of his anchorage at Schooneveld, since it was supposed that having an inferior force he was unlikely to come out to do battle with the Allied fleet. It was recognised that to attempt to enter the Schooneveld channel would be an extremely risky manoeuvre, since while the shoals were extremely familiar to the Dutch, they were not well known to the English, and were inadequately charted. Spragge was disgusted at the failure to get reliable information. Observing 'that the banks of Flanders are laid between two and 2½ leagues further off than they are set down on the cards', he went on to remark in his journal:

> In times of peace we ought to employ some able men to the finding the truth and danger of these banks. The difficulties and dangers that were often apprehended of these banks saved the enemy's utter ruin ... In the whole no entire victory is ever to be had of the enemy except we are well acquainted with their ports, so as

---

5   *Ibid.*, p.31.
6   Fox, *Great Ships*, pp.110–112.
7   Anderson, *Third Dutch War*, p.316.

to be able to pursue them into them, it being an easy work to destroy an enemy disheartened and beaten.[8]

In spite of the dangers, it was agreed that an assault should be launched against de Ruyter's fleet as it lay in its anchorage. Taking a leaf out of the Dutch admiral's book, it was also resolved that a force of lighter vessels and fireships should precede the fleet. This was not so much to take advantage of surprise, as de Ruyter had done at Solebay, but rather to prevent the Dutch escaping into Flushing, as the Allied fleet approached, by using the southern exit from the anchorage. Anderson described this:

> The Schooneveld is a wide channel running approximately SW and NE outside the shoals off Walcheren. At its southern end the Wielingen channel leads to Flushing, while to the NE a continuation, the Steendiep, runs past the Banjaard shoal towards the mouth of the Maas. Along its outer side there are a series of banks with for the most part some 6 fathoms or more, but with occasional shallow patches, some even drying at low water. The first of these, the Oosterbank, is about 9 miles from the corresponding shoal to the SE, but towards the Banjaard the channel narrows to 2 miles or less.[9]

Apart from the refusal of his wish to have Holmes as a flag officer, the command arrangements of the English fleet were more or less to Rupert's satisfaction. His Vice Admiral of the Red Squadron was Sir John Harman, with Sir John Chicheley, who was rather less experienced, as Rear Admiral. Supporting Spragge in the Blue Squadron was Sir John Kempthorne as Vice Admiral and the Earl of Ossory as Rear Admiral. The latter post was intended for Sir John Narbrough, but he had not returned from Tangier in time. D'Estrées commanded the French fleet, designated as the White Squadron; des Ardents and de Grancey were the *chefs d'escadre*. The Allied fleet was composed of 86 ships carrying a total of 4,812 guns. The order of battle was, however, changed: the White Squadron was to be stationed in the centre, with the Red Squadron in the lead. This was no doubt to prevent the kind of misunderstanding that had led to the separation of the fleet at Solebay. Spragge, for his part, was disapproving of the change, much later complaining that, with the Red Squadron in the van, due to the length of the line he could not see the signals Rupert made; he thought that the change was 'quite contrary to any custom ever used at sea before, and may prove of ill consequence to us. I know not any reason he has for it except being singular and positive.'[10]

De Ruyter's fleet, once the Zeelanders had joined, consisted of 52 ships carrying 3,171 guns. It was organised in three squadrons. Tromp commanded the van, with his flag in the *Gouden Leeuw;* Schramm, his Vice Admiral, was in the *Pacificatie*, and his third flag officer (known as the Schout bij Nacht) was de Haen, aboard the 80 gun *Hollandia* (not to be confused with

---

8   *Ibid.*, p.319.
9   *Ibid.*, p.30.
10   *Ibid.*, p.327.

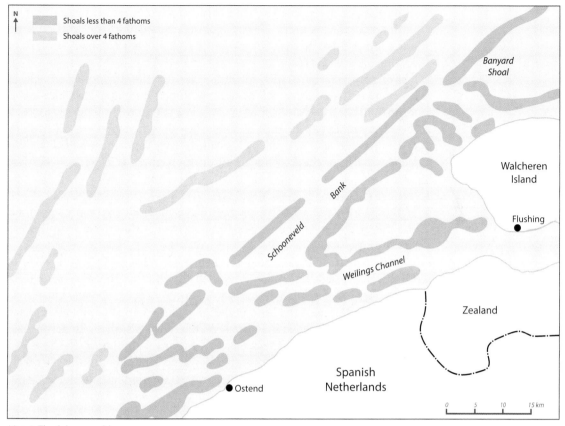

Map 4 The Schooneveld.

the *Groot Hollandia*, of 68 guns or the *Klein Hollandia* of 58 guns). Second-in-command of the Centre Squadron was Aert van Nes, with his flag in the *Eendracht*, and there were two other flag officers: de Liefde aboard the *Vrijheid* and Jan van Nes in the *Maagd van Dordrecht*. Banckert commanded the rear squadron aboard the *Walcheren*, with Evertsen in the *Zierikzee* and Vlugh in the *Wapen van Enkhuisen*.

Rupert sailed with the Allied fleet on 20 May, anchoring off the North Foreland on the following evening. Next day he steered for the Dutch coast, anchoring some 15 miles north-north-west off Ostend, from where he could see de Ruyter's fleet at anchor in the Schooneveld. On May 23 he took up a position nine miles SW of the Dutch, and there he waited for the weather to improve; for several days a southwesterly gale had brought high winds, fog and rain. On 27 May he called a council of war, where it was resolved to attack the enemy at the first opportunity, and if de Ruyter retired into Flushing, to anchor in the Schooneveld.

When, next day, the weather moderated, the attack began. The fleet weighed anchor at 10:00 a.m. at high water, and began to move towards the enemy with the wind west-north-west. At this moment de Ruyter was himself holding a council of war aboard the *Zeven Provincien*. Apart from the long-running enmity of de Ruyter and Tromp, there had been issues arising between other Dutch admirals, but they now met in a spirit of reconciliation, determined to win a battle which they regarded as critical for the future of their country. Following this, for some time de Ruyter made no move himself; but he then surprised the Allies by offering battle instead of retiring towards Flushing.

For some reason it was not until 1:00 p.m. that firing began, still at long range. It seemed to the Dutch that Rupert had adopted a half-moon formation, but this is probably due to the fact that Rupert and Spragge closed the enemy more quickly than d'Estrées. The detached group of Allied ships came first into action, principally against Tromp, on whose squadron also fell the attack of the Red Squadron. In the centre, de Grancey's division, instead of concentrating on de Ruyter's Squadron, closed with the leading ships of Banckert's rear squadron. The effect was to leave only about a dozen of the enemy to the whole of Spragge's Blue Squadron; even more important was that had also left only about 10 or 12 French ships to face de Ruyter's squadron.[11]

When it became clear that the Dutch intended to fight, the ships of the advanced detachment were recalled to return to the squadrons from which they had originally been drawn. However, since the detachment was concentrated towards the head of the Allied line they could not all get back to rejoin their respective squadrons. As the range closed, de Ruyter formed his battle line on the port tack, heading north east-by-north. As the Allied fleet neared the Dutch line Rupert also turned into line on the port tack. Preceding Rupert's division, that of Harman was soon heavily engaged with Tromp's van division. Harman's flagship, the *London*, was involved in a fierce duel with the *Pacificatie*, aboard which Schramm was killed early in the exchange. Rupert, in the *Royal Charles*, concentrated his fire on Tromp's flagship, the *Gouden Leeuw*. Ahead of the *Royal Charles*, the *Royal Katherine*, commanded by George Legge, endeavoured to bring up a fireship, which grappled with the *Jupiter* before sinking alongside. Legge wrote in his journal: 'Whereupon I immediately sent my boats with men and took the man of war. But her rigging, masts and sails so much shot and seven feet water in hold, our men left her and most of the Dutch.'[12] The fighting was at this point so fierce that Legge did not know whether the *Jupiter* sank, or what became of her. In fact, she seems to have been able to get back into port.

In his duel with the *Gouden Leeuw*, Rupert was frustrated to find that the *Royal Charles* was heeling over so far in the wind as to make it impossible to use her lowest tier of guns. Fortunately he was supported by the French 56-gun ship, *Conquérant*, and between them they so damaged Tromp's flagship as to necessitate his shifting his flag to the 54-gun *Prins te Paard*. Aboard the *Conquérant* her captain, de Tivas, was killed during these exchanges.

By reason of the way in which the Allied fleet had deployed, de Ruyter's squadron had been much less heavily engaged, and at about 3;00 p.m. he decided to tack with the intention of cutting off the rearmost portion of the Allies. This manoeuvre brought his squadron into the middle of the French squadron. Banckert, in the rear, was close enough to be able to see what

11   *Ibid.*, p.33.
12   *Ibid.*, pp.300–301.

was happening, and to conform to de Ruyter's signals, but Tromp was out of sight, and a yacht was sent to tell him of the movement. De Ruyter's bold move was only partly successful; the leading French division, and some ships of the centre division, including the *Reine*, d'Estrées flagship, remained to windward. De Ruyter was able to weather the rest of the division, but de Grancey and Spragge, in the rear, were able to avoid the danger by tacking as well.[13]

De Ruyter's manoeuvre gave the French an opportunity for a great success, when the *Foudroyant*, forced out of line by the *Zeven Provincien*, collided with the Dutch *Deventer*, which had lost her main topsail. Some of the French boarded the *Deventer*, occupying her forecastle, but Gabaret, the *Foudroyant*'s captain, missed his chance, and instead of reinforcing his boarders, he dropped anchor to let the tide take the Dutch ship clear. The *Deventer*'s captain led a counter-attack, and drove the French boarders back to their ship.

De Ruyter and Banckertt now headed southward, towards de Grancey and Spragge, putting the Blue Squadron in serious danger. Spragge, in his journal, lamented that the *Royal Prince* was exposed to both Dutch squadrons:

Having no sight of our Red Squadron, the wind then veering to the NE, I stood off about half an hour. It being half an hour past five, I tacked and stood in again just a-weather of all the Dutch fleet, receiving my friends de Ruyter, Banckert and most of all the enemy's broadsides within musket shot, seconded only by the *Cambridge*, who was much disabled.[14]

De Ruyter, however, now turned back northwards to go to the support of Tromp, followed by Banckert. Once united, the whole Dutch fleet again stood to the southward, giving Spragge the chance of a crack at Tromp, whom he had promised would be brought back dead or alive. For some reason he had fixed in his mind the notion that Tromp must be his principal target. By now the Dutch Lieutenant Admiral had been obliged to shift his flag again, the *Prince te Paard* having received serious damage in the engagement with the Red Squadron in the course of which her captain was killed; his flag now flew in the *Amsterdam*. At least, it did for a while, until during his action against Spragge the *Amsterdam* was dismasted, and Tromp moved again, this time to the *Komeetster*. His Rear Admiral, de Haen, was also obliged to shift his flag as a result of the damage suffered by the *Hollandia*, switching to the *Provincie van Utrecht* until she too was heavily damaged whereupon he shifted to the *Wakende Kraan*.

Although both fleets were now heading in a generally southerly direction, both their battle lines were in considerable disorder. They continued in this way until darkness fell at about 10:00 p.m. At this time the wind was in the north-north-east, and the Allied fleet steered west-north-west until it was safely clear of the shoals. Throughout the battle all the captains in the Allied fleet had constantly in their minds the risk that they were running. As Legge

---

13 *Ibid.*, p.33.
14 *Ibid.*, p.320.

observed: 'The place where we fought was very dangerous, for we feared more the losing of our ships upon the sands than we did losing our ships and lives in fight with the enemy.'[15]

Neither side had lost any major ships in the course of the battle, although each was obliged to send back into port three ships more seriously damaged than could be repaired at sea. The English *Cambridge* and *Resolution*, and the French *Conquérant* were sent home; on the Dutch side the *Prins te Paard*, the *Zuiderhuis* and the *Deventer* went in for repairs, though the last named was accidentally wrecked on the way. Casualties on each side seem to have been surprisingly light, though no accurate figures are known. On the other hand, the losses in senior officers were disproportionately great. In addition to Schramm, the Dutch lost Vlugh and four captains killed: these were van Bergen of the *Prins te Paard*, van Nassau of the *Provincie van Utrecht*, de Boer of the *Wapen van Holland* and Meeganck of the *Damiate* (possibly a fireship). On the Allied side five captains were killed: in addition to de Tivas of the *Conquérant*, Fowlis of the *Lion*, Werden of the *Henrietta*, Finch of the *York* and Tempest of the *Sweepstakes* also died. Total English losses were said by a French writer to be 300 killed and wounded, and the French about the same, though these figures are not to be relied on. Haddock apparently put the English losses at between 400 and 500 men. So far as can be guessed at, the Dutch casualties were not greatly different from those of the Allies.

Since the situation of the two fleets was not greatly altered by the battle, the allies having retired from the dangers of the Dutch shoals, and the Dutch having returned to the safety of the Schooneveld, it may be said that the battle was indecisive. Yet taken overall, the balance of advantage was decidedly in de Ruyter's favour. He had been heavily outnumbered, but had held his own, and had achieved his objective of preventing any landing on the Dutch coast; not unreasonably he felt able to report to William that 'so far the victory (God be praised) is on the side of this state, and of your Highness.'[16] He was under no illusion, however, that a further battle would almost certainly be necessary if he was to thwart any invasion.

It was by no means clear to Rupert just how much damage had been inflicted on the Dutch fleet. He claimed in his report to the King that 'the enemy had a considerable loss, which they will not easily repair.' Rather more accurately, he reported that his own losses were 'very inconsiderable.' He praised the French, who 'behaved themselves very bravely,' and also Spragge, who 'maintained the fight with so much courage and resolution, that had it not been for fear of the shoals, we had driven them into their harbours.' He ended his report with the hope that 'his Majesty will be satisfied, that considering the place we engaged in, and the sands, there was as much done as could be expected.'[17] He was, perhaps, conscious that in fact not a great deal had been accomplished.

Spragge, in his journal, was a good deal more realistic:

---

15 *Ibid.*, p.301.
16 Blok, p.334.
17 Anderson, *Third Dutch War*, pp.387–388.

It proved a very ill fighting place for so great a number of ships. And in truth as ill fought of our side as ever yet I saw. Whatever resolutions or designs the enemy had by lying at Schooneveld, I am persuaded our ill conduct and most notorious cowardice will make them take new measures, and instead of being in their own defence before, they will now (with great reason) be the offenders and seekers.[18]

Reviewing the outcome of the battle, Peter Padfield wrote that Rupert's tactics had been 'a disaster, carrying all the disadvantages for gunnery of the melée without the compensating advantage of isolating and overwhelming individual enemy groups.' He noted that Rupert, in spite of his numerical superiority at the head of the Red Squadron, had been unable to break up Tromp's Squadron, while the performance of d'Estrées had been 'lamentable.'[19] Rupert has had two recent biographers; one of these, Charles Spencer, alone among historians of the battle, claims it as a victory, a view based on an inaccurate assessment of the Dutch losses. The other, Frank Kitson, notes that the Allies had neither destroyed de Ruyter's fleet, nor bottled it up, and that therefore no strategic advantage had been gained; this is a view which is hard to dispute.[20]

As he lay at anchor on the Oosterbank, Rupert had not only to deal with the problem of making repairs at sea, but also with grave difficulties of supply. His fleet had already been at sea for a month, and it was obvious that he could not long remain on the Dutch coast. For the moment he stayed in place, kept under observation by de Ruyter, who was perfectly aware of the limitations of endeavouring to patch up warships at sea. He was awaiting an opportunity to launch an attack on the Allied fleet, which was something for which Tromp 'was again thirsting with all his heart and soul.'[21]

Such opportunity seemed to Spragge to have arisen on 1 June, as he wrote in his journal:

Had the enemy come down on us this day, our fleet be anchored intermixed, they might have caught us in great disorder and have made us generally to have cut. For which reason and to prevent such surprise you ought always to have your scouts out and your fleet always, if room, to anchor in the line you must sail, and always to sail in the line of battle, if by the wind. If large, and sea room, the squadron that is to have the van of the battle ought to sail all abreast, and to make the headmost; the General's squadron to follow in the same order; the Rear Admiral's squadron to do the like and to keep a fine distance.[22]

Generally speaking, Spragge had no great opinion of Rupert's tactical sense.

---

18 *Ibid.*, p.320.
19 Padfield, p.99.
20 Charles Spencer, *Prince Rupert: The Last Cavalier* (London: Wiedenfeld and Nicolson, 2007), pp.352–353; Frank Kitson, *Prince Rupert: Admiral and General-at Sea* (London: Constable, 1998), p.269.
21 Blok, p.334.
22 Anderson, *Third Dutch War*, p.321.

However, it looks very much as though Rupert, for his part, was prepared to take advice, since on 1 June he redeployed the fleet to take account of the issues raised by Spragge when he visited the flagship on that day. The Red Squadron was now anchored at the southern end of the fleet, nearest to the coast, with the French squadron in the centre and the Blue Squadron furthest out to sea. The divisions were arranged in nine parallel lines, running north-west to south-east; in each the flagship was in the centre of the line. It was intended that these be half a mile apart, but in fact the gaps between them were nearly twice this.[23] Meanwhile Rupert, extremely put out by the performance of the *Royal Charles*, decided to shift his flag to the *Royal Sovereign*. This he did on 3 June, and Haddock, and the second captain of the *Royal Charles*, Anthony Young, accompanied him. Very early next day Haddock arranged the transfer of no less than 250 men into the *Royal Sovereign*; even allowing for the importance of the commander-in-chief's flagship being fully manned, this does seem a lot.[24]

The question now for the Allies was what to do next. There was a pretty general distaste for the idea of engaging the Dutch again in the shoals of the Schooneveld. Haddock spoke for most of the Allied captains in a letter which he wrote to the Navy Commissioners after the battle of 28 May: 'we have now very bad weather, wind at NSW, blowing hard. I am glad we are out of the Schooneveld. I believe we shall not attack the Dutch in that narrow hole again.'[25]

On the morning of 4 June Spragge set off from his flagship to confer with Rupert. The wind had changed to the north-east, which had alerted Rupert to the possibility that de Ruyter might take advantage of this to come out in the night, and he apparently stayed up all night to be prepared for this. The oarsmen in Spragge's boat were going to have a long pull. Spragge reckoned that the distance to the *Royal Sovereign* was at least 10 miles. Even if this was an overestimate, the Allied squadrons were evidently widely scattered. While Spragge was on his way, de Ruyter took the decision about what to do out of the Allies' hands. Soon after 11:00 a.m. the Dutch fleet got under way. Although Spragge could see the Dutch coming out he continued on his way to the *Royal Sovereign*, where Rupert had little to say to him other than that he should return at once to his own flagship, which he reached at about 2:00 p.m.[26]

Spragge's Blue Squadron was supposed to lead the Allied line, and it seemed to Rupert that, as Spragge made his way back to the *Prince*, the Dutch would arrive before the Blue Squadron was able to do so. He took the risky decision to sail the Red Squadron through the French in order himself to take the lead. Not having been able to explain to d'Estrées what he intended, the manoeuvre caused a good deal of confusion, as the ships of the Red and White Squadrons became intermingled.

23 Kitson, p.270.
24 Anderson, *Third Dutch War*, p.336.
25 Quoted in G.J. Marcus, *A Naval History of England: Vol. I, The Formative Years* (Boston, Mass.: Little, Brown and Co., 1961), p.170.
26 Anderson, *Third Dutch War*, pp.321–322.

A depiction of the English Warship *Sovereign*. Originally launched as the *Sovereign of the Seas* in 1637, the vessel was, in part, funded by the 'Ship Money' tax of Charles I. It served as Blake's flagship and saw action in all three Anglo-Dutch Wars. Its sad end came in January 1697, when laid up at Chatham Dockyard, she was burnt to the waterline in an accident. (Private collection)

Spragge, meanwhile, had got his squadron in order and set off to take the lead. As he neared the Dutch, his obsession with Tromp again surfaced. He wrote in his journal:

> Tromp, whose squadron had the van, being very impatient, fired a gun to stay for him; you would have thought by his vapouring and fierceness we were to be eaten alive. Our ships astern being in very great disorder, I continued sailing, hoping to bring them into a good line; but seeing no hopes [of it], and Tromp's vapour being still in my head, I shortened sail. The gent[leman's] courage seemed somewhat moderated, that instead of eating us all alive he very cowardly lay large gunshot to the windward, never daring to come at nearer distance.[27]

The general action began in the van at about 4:00 p.m., when Tromp's squadron engaged that of Spragge, but it was not until an hour or so later that the other two Allied squadrons were in action. De Ruyter in the *Zeven Provincien*, at first headed for the *Royal Sovereign*, but once within musket shot turned away, and continued to fire at long range. De Ruyter's biographer records that Rupert more than once hoisted the red flag as a signal for a

---

27   *Ibid.*, p.322.

general attack, but each time hauled down again, which perplexed de Ruyter, who exclaimed: 'Is he going mad, or what's wrong with him?'[28] Dutch and English accounts differ as to how the engagement between de Ruyter and Rupert progressed. Rupert claimed that the Dutch Admiral 'sprang his luff and closed his wind as much as he possibly could, going off on a sudden for good and all.' The Dutch maintained that it was Rupert who turned away, firing his stern guns instead of his broadside. Haddock recorded in his journal: 'We kept our luff; they did likewise the same; would not come close to us.'[29] Since de Ruyter's aim was simply to frustrate any Allied attempt to effect a landing of troops, it is not surprising that he was being careful to avoid needless losses, and had given orders to his commanders accordingly. He is said to have remarked: 'They will fight with me when I please, but I won't when they please.'

Thus the battle continued at long range into the evening. Even Tromp, to Spragge's frustration, continued to stand off, and 'did not once dare to make a proffer with any of his fireships.' In spite of this, the Dutch succeeded in inflicting considerable damage on their opponents; at 4:45 p.m. the *Prince's* main topsail was shot to pieces, and at 6:00 Spragge's carpenter came to tell him that he had five feet of water in the hold. Haddock recorded that, although not knowing what damage had been done to the enemy, 'on our parts we lost two fireships; shattered our ships, many of them, in hull, masts and rigging.' Two captains had been killed: White of the *Warspite* and Sadlington of the *Crown*.[30]

The heaviest fighting had been in the van. Sweers, the second in command, in the *Olifant*, had come into range sooner than Tromp, and suffered so much damage that he was obliged to turn out of line, a fact which led afterwards to a furious dispute between the two men. Sweers had only rejoined the fleet after the first Schooneveld battle. Other Dutch ships to suffer serious damage were the *Voorsichtheid* and the *Waesdorp*. Astern of the *Royal Sovereign*, Legge's *Royal Katherine* was badly damaged, in part, he claimed, because several English and most of the French ships did not keep as close to the wind as they could while he had kept a better wind:

> We engaged with de Ruyter and most of his squadron from four in the afternoon till nine at night, having about 30 men killed and between 60 and 70 desperately wounded and all our masts, yards, rigging and sails disabled and several of our guns and carriages broke and disabled and likewise all the shot we had in the ship for the guns on the two upper decks spent.[31]

The *Prince* had been sufficiently seriously damaged for Spragge to notify his Vice Admiral and Rear Admiral of the possibility that he might have to turn out of line. He kept his pumps going to keep the water level down, but at 10:00 p.m. was obliged to leave the line. The firing continued until after

---

28   Blok, p.335.
29   Anderson, *Third Dutch War*, p.336.
30   *Ibid.*
31   *Ibid.*, p.303.

midnight when de Ruyter, correctly supposing that he had done enough to achieve his basic objective, tacked and steered for home. The records of exactly what the Allies then did are contradictory; it seems that it was some time before they tacked. At about 5:00 a.m. next morning, with the Allied fleet now 25 or 30 miles from Solebay, Rupert convened a council of war. In view of a general shortage of ammunition, and the badly damaged state of some of the ships, it was decided not to anchor there but to proceed to the Nore. The fleet anchored for the night off the Gunfleet; over the next few days the most seriously damaged ships went into the Medway. De Ruyter, by the evening of 5 June, was once more safely ensconced in the Schooneveld.

Spragge felt that an opportunity had been missed:

> We had in this battle great want of order, no man well knowing his station, which must inevitably be a ruin to that army so governed. Had the body of our fleet tacked on de Ruyter, he being very weak in that part of the line, we should probably have got the battle. The strength and their hopes was in the van of their fleet, which was commanded by Tromp ... We very tamely let him go, till he was out of reach, and then we made as if we had a mind to follow.[32]

No ship had been lost on either side, though several had been seriously damaged. There appears to be no accurate record of the total casualties suffered by each side though the Amsterdam contingent which made up half the Dutch fleet, had 216 men killed and 258 wounded. The rest of the Dutch fleet probably had fewer casualties. If it had been more or less indecisive in a tactical sense, it was plainly another strategic victory for de Ruyter, since there was now no immediate prospect of the Allies being able to launch an invasion with the Dutch fleet still intact. It would be some weeks before sufficient of the damaged Allied ships were repaired, at least to the point of making them battleworthy.

Although there was again some dissatisfaction that the French contribution had been disappointing, one of Rupert's biographers notes that he and d'Estrées were still on speaking terms. Rupert, in his official report, made no reference to the performance of the French squadron, and nor did d'Estrées make any complaint about Rupert's leadership. After this battle Louis wrote to Rupert to express his gratitude 'for the manner in which you have used the Comte d'Estrées and those in his charge.'[33] D'Estrées did, however, complained bitterly of Spragge's conduct. On the Dutch side, Tromp's complaint about Sweers was sufficiently serious to lead de Ruyter to commission an investigation. He sent three flag officers from other squadrons to inspect the *Olifant*; having done so, they unanimously concluded that Tromp's complaints were without foundation. The Prince of Orange suggested that Sweers might be transferred to Banckert's squadron, and be replaced by Evertsen, but de Ruyter, who thought that the dispute was due to 'old grievances', decided to leave things as they were.

---

32 *Ibid.*, pp.322–323.
33 Kitson, p.273.

8

The Fleets at Sea Again

While the fleet was refitting, it was once again necessary to rethink the strategy that must now be pursued, and on 11 June Charles, accompanied by James, came down to the Nore to discuss the position with Rupert. On 14 June Rupert went ashore for a further meeting in London, where next day James formally resigned from his post as Lord High Admiral, and as Generalissimo of the operations against the United Provinces. This meant that Rupert could now be given a new commission entitling him to appoint and remove officers in the fleet. It also meant that something must be done about the post of Lord High Admiral, and Charles decided to put the office into commission; Rupert was the first Commissioner. However, the King reserved certain powers to himself, and Frank Kitson has suggested that 'in effect he made himself his own Lord High Admiral.'[1] With the unofficial help of his brother, he intended to exercise control over major policy decisions.

Rupert returned to the fleet on 21 June. The refitting had been seriously delayed by the lack of stores. The Dutch, meanwhile, had been keeping an eye on the Allied fleet ever since a frigate had reported on 9 June that it had retired into the Thames. De Ruyter sent a detachment of 12 ships to reconnoitre further, under the command of de Haen. The latter returned on 15 June with information that the Allied fleet was indeed refitting in the Thames and the Medway, and that an army of 30,000 men was being assembled for an invasion. It was in fact true that an expeditionary force was being prepared, although it was actually to consist only of 10,000 men, under the command of Count Friedrich Schomberg. De Ruyter was at this time under strong pressure to effect a landing of troops himself in either England or France, in the hope that this would do something to lessen the threat to the besieged fortress of Maastricht. De Ruyter did not consider such an operation to be practicable, but he was willing at least to make a demonstration. He emerged from his secure anchorage in the Schooneveld with a fleet of 100 vessels, of which 55 were ships of the line, and appeared at the mouth of the Thames before the Allies were ready to sail. The effort proved abortive, however, due

---

1   Kitson, p.274.

to increasing sickness in the Dutch fleet, and he withdrew to the mouth of the Maas on 29 June, before 10 days later returning to his former bolt hole in the Schooneveld.[2]

Aboard his flagship, Rupert was becoming extremely frustrated, particularly as a result of the delays on the part of the victuallers, but also because of the lack of any clear instructions. He wrote to Arlington on 3 July:

> If his Majesty has any design for 4,000 men he must tell us what we shall do ... My opinion is to go out as soon and as strong as we can and to fight the enemy's fleet, if they can be at sea; and this is the opinion of most of the fleet. If he will give me any further commands I shall most humbly receive them, but to desire with all duty that they shall be in writing.[3]

He followed this up next day with an angry note to Arlington setting out his demands to be placed before the King:

> That I may have my commission as soon as may be.
>
> That his Majesty and his Royal Highness be pleased to name the ships designed for this fleet, and that none be diverted for convoys, guard of coast et cetera.
>
> That I may have power to command all the yards, victuals, stores and what shall be necessary to set out the fleet.
>
> That I may have power from His Majesty to punish all misdemeanours according to the custom of war and the Seas.
>
> And a power to sink, burn destroy or take any ships, men or country in possession of the Dutch.[4]

With reports before him that de Ruyter was now anchored at the Wielings off Sluys, Rupert saw as his immediate task the making of some demonstration there. If that did not bring the Dutch out, he proposed to go north along the coast to lure de Ruyter out with the threat of landings. On 6 July he announced his intention of putting to sea in two days' time, by which date the fleet would be ready to sail. There had in the meantime been a number of changes in the fleet, most notably the removal of Richard Haddock from the *Royal Sovereign*. This was due, as Spragge laconically noted in his journal, to his 'not being well approved of in the last battles.' Haddock was replaced by Sir William Reeves, of the *Edgar*, with Captain John Wetwang as his second captain. John Narbrough had now finally rejoined the fleet, and was appointed as the 'Eldest Captain' aboard Ossory's flagship, the *St Michael*, of which he took command on 1 July.

Preparing the ship to be ready to go to sea, Narbrough mustered the crew of the *St Michael* on 6 July, finding a total of 701 men and boys aboard her. This total included 134 soldiers and 120 'trouncers' and tradesmen 'which never were at sea and [are] unfit for sea service.'[5]

---

2   Anderson, *Third Dutch War*, p.42.
3   Richmond, p.184.
4   Kitson, pp.275–276.
5   Anderson, *Third Dutch War*, p.340.

That day Charles arrived again for a visit to the fleet at the head of a particularly high-powered party, which included not only his brother James but also Count Schomberg, Arlington and the Duke of Buckingham, with several other members of the Privy Council. A Council meeting was held, and Spragge summarised its conclusions: 'The question was put how the enemy was to be attempted and how to draw them out of the Schooneveld. The result was to attempt landing at the Texel; that and their East India fleet would draw them out to fight us.'[6] Next day a further meeting was held, at which it was decided that the force of 4,000 troops immediately available should be embarked. Rupert, however, was insistent that before an attempt was made at landing them, the Dutch fleet must first be disposed of.

Corbett was of the view that this had always also been the King's view; Richmond commented on the odd way in which Charles had been dealing with this:

> If it be correct that the King had throughout been of the same opinion and that the real intention was to use the army as a threat to force the enemy to come to see, it is difficult to understand why this should not have been fully explained to the commander in chief; for if one thing be necessary in a campaign it is that the motives of those who direct the strategy should be clearly conveyed to the commander in the field and no less that the conduct of the operation should be left to him. But this essential information was being withheld and at the same time no freedom of action was being accorded.[7]

Arriving at a clear decision as to the strategy to be adopted involved a lot of discussion. At yet another council of war on 16 July Rupert got his way, and it was agreed that the troops, once embarked, should be sent to Yarmouth until de Ruyter had been dealt with. Significantly, it was also expressly agreed 'not to attack them in the Schooneveld until further order from the King upon no pretence whatever.'[8] That this followed a direct order from Charles is made clear in the text of the resolutions passed by the council, which refer to the King having 'further knowledge of the treaty and his Majesty's other affairs.'

The plan agreed upon was for the Allied fleet to show itself off the Schooneveld and then to proceed to the Texel 'whither it is to be hoped the enemy will be drawn (and give the opportunity of fighting them where there is sea room) for the preventing a descent upon their coast and securing the East India ships now expected home.'[9] Next day, a final conclusion having been reached, the fleet put to sea, accompanied by Charles and James for some way before they returned to London.

On 18 July the fleet stood out of the Gunfleet, and came to anchor between the Long Sand Head and the Shipwash sands where, later, there was an unfortunate incident which Narbrough recorded in his journal:

---

6   *Ibid.*, p.324.
7   Richmond, pp.184–185.
8   Anderson, *Third Dutch War*, p.326.
9   Kitson, p.277.

> This afternoon the *Greyhound* frigate came into the fleet with a St George flag flying at the main top mast head, Monsieur Schomberg being aboard of her, General of the land forces which are raised against the United Provinces. When the *Greyhound* came near the Admiral, Prince Rupert fired at her and caused her to strike her flag, and put the captain of her in irons for wearing a flag.[10]

The captain's defence was that he had been ordered by the King to follow Schomberg's instructions, and when told to hoist the flag he had done so under protest. Rupert, his temper having cooled, pardoned him. The incident led to lasting ill feeling on Schomberg's part, who wrote to Arlington to complain of Rupert's conduct: 'I am afraid he does not take the advice of the wisest, and that he allows himself to be governed by his former page, Sir W Reeves.'[11]

The Allied fleet eventually set off across the North Sea on 19 July in accordance with the decisions reached, the troop transports having been sent to Yarmouth, and anchored off the Schooneveld on 21 July, behind which as usual lay the Dutch fleet. De Ruyter's orders were, notwithstanding the odds, to attack in order to prevent any landing. Next morning both fleets weighed anchor, the Allied fleet moving off to the north, followed by de Ruyter, who was soon gaining on the rearmost squadron, that of Spragge. The wind, which had hitherto been west-north-west, now backed, just as Spragge was ordered by Rupert to tack, in the hope of weathering the enemy. This isolated Spragge to windward of the rest of the Allied fleet and de Ruyter, seizing the opportunity, closed on the Blue Squadron. In order to keep clear of Spragge's ships the Red Squadron had been obliged to bear away, thus falling further to leeward, while the French were still farther off. Spragge, ultimately, had no choice but to retire; he crossly described these events in his journal:

> While we stood to the northward, the enemy followed us, which was till 12 o'clock, at which time the Prince made the sign for the van of the fleet to tack, where I then was; the French in another line to the leeward of me. I tacked and stood to the southward; the enemy's van at the same time did the same thing. At 1 o'clock the Prince sent me his Lieutenant, by name _____, to tack and use my own discretion, which I took in writing under his hand. In the time of this tack the wind veered from the NW to the SW, so that from lying WSW by the stem, by the time I fetched the length of the Red, I could lie but SSE on which the enemy re-tacked and lay WNW with their larboard tacks on board, in so much that I could not get the wind of a quarter of the enemy's fleet. Our Red Squadron, instead of keeping the wind the best they could, they (from the time the sign was made for me to tack to the southward of the enemy) bore away near three leagues to the leeward.[12]

Spragge was extremely critical of the way the fleet had been handled, observing that if the Red Squadron 'had sprang their luff again all along,

---

10 Anderson, *Third Dutch War*, p.342.
11 Corbett, p.34; Kitson, p.278.
12 Anderson, *Third Dutch War*, pp.327–328.

I'm sure we had engaged the enemy, who were very inconsiderable to us.' He pointed the finger at Harman, the Vice Admiral of the Red Squadron, who would be 'best able to tell if there had been slackness or neglect.' He added: 'I was so great a distance from the Red that I cannot say much to it, only this much I say, that that was done by us I never saw done before, nor, I hope, never will again.'[13]

Spragge, who had insisted on getting Rupert's instructions in writing, seems not to have been so keen to put his own orders in that way, as Narbrough recorded:

> My Lord Ossory sent his lieutenant, Henry Carverth, on board Sir Edward Spragge, to know of him if he should keep his wind or bear away to our fleet. Sir Edward sent him word that he should bear towards our fleet before him; this order Lieutenant Carverth brought from Sir Edward Spragge by word of mouth; Sir Edward would not give any order from under his hand.[14]

Putting the best face on it that he could, Narbrough reckoned that the Dutch had missed an opportunity, 'having the weather gage of us and smooth water and night towards.' The Dutch view was very different; the Allies had retreated from an inferior fleet.

Part of the problem was deploying the French or White Squadron in the middle of the line with the Red in the van. It might have served to achieve greater control over what were suspected to be reluctant allies, but as Spragge remarked, 'many inconveniences may and do daily happen by putting the French in the middle.'

There is no doubt that the Allied fleet was much the stronger, although until R.C. Anderson edited his *Journals and Narratives of the Third Dutch War* in 1946 the exact composition of the two fleets at this point was extremely uncertain; Julian Corbett, writing 38 years earlier, noted that 'no authentic list of either fleet has come to light.' Anderson, however, by careful research, was able to conclude with some confidence that the two English squadrons consisted of 56 ships of the line with 3,558 guns. Probably the Red Squadron accounted for 29 ships of 1,870 guns and the Blue Squadron for 27 ships of 1,690 guns. The French squadron was composed of 30 ships carrying 1,828 guns.

In Rupert's Red Squadron, the Vice Admiral was Sir John Harman (aboard the *Charles*), and the Rear Admiral was Sir John Chicheley (aboard the *London*). In the Blue Squadron, Spragge's Vice Admiral remained Sir John Kempthorne (*St Andrew*) and his Rear Admiral the Earl of Ossory (*St Michael*). D'Estrées's second in command was now the Marquis de Martel (*Royale Thérèse*) with des Ardents (*Terrible*) as the senior *chef d'escadre*.

De Ruyter had 60 ships of the line, carrying a total of 3,667 guns. Tromp, as before, led the van in the *Gouden Leeuw*, supported by Sweers in the *Olifant* and de Haen in the *Hollandia*. De Ruyter's second in command was Aert van Nes in the *Eendracht*; the other two admirals of the centre squadron were

---

13   *Ibid.*, p.328.
14   *Ibid.*, p.346.

de Liefde in the *Vrijheid* and Jan van Nes (*Maagd van Dordrecht*). Banckert again led the rear squadron aboard the *Walcheren*, supported by Cornelis Evertsen the Younger (*Zierikzee*), Star (*Groeningen*) and Bruynsvelt (*Prins Hendrik Casimir*).

After the battle that never happened on 22 July, the Allied fleet made its way slowly north-eastwards up the Dutch coast. Rupert convened a council of war on the morning of 24 July. Spragge noted the decision:

> It was resolved on sending scouts to the Vlie and to the Texel, to discover what number of ships of the enemy's, and the fleet not to appear very near till the scouts returned. And in case any considerable number of ships were there, to attempt the destroying of them. In the meanwhile to keep five or six leagues off from the shore.[15]

By 25 July, when the Allied fleet anchored off the Texel and the Vlie, it seems that the disadvantage of locating d'Estrées in the centre had by now been recognised. That night, while the fleet lay at anchor on the Broad Fourteens, the Red Squadron was located between the other two. Rupert now felt the need to seek further instructions, and on 27 July sent a letter to Arlington raising three questions. First, should he now send for the troop transports patiently waiting at Yarmouth? Secondly, if news could be had of the movements of the Dutch East India fleet, should he go after this tempting target? Finally if de Ruyter still declined to come out from behind the Schooneveld, should he attack him there? The best season for campaigning was coming to an end; whatever was to be done, it would be well if it was done quickly. It was particularly frustrating, therefore, that it was not until 9 August that he received an answer to his request for instructions.

By then the situation had changed considerably. De Ruyter, in response to orders from the Prince of Orange to maintain contact with the Allied fleet, put to sea on 28 July. He went no further than Scheveningen, and after calling a Council of War reported that the collective view was that it would be best to remain off the mouth of the Maas, which would more or less enable him to cover the coastline from the Texel to Walcheren. By now, however, the fate of the valuable East India fleet, which was never far from the minds of both commanders and their respective governments, was beginning to influence strategic thinking. De Ruyter's move on 28 July had in part been prompted by concern for the East Indiamen, and on 2 August the Prince of Orange arrived at the fleet aboard a fishing smack for a conference with de Ruyter. This appears to have been the only occasion upon which he paid a visit to the fleet in his official capacity.[16] His object was:

> … to try to convince him of the necessity of a battle as soon as possible if the East India fleet was to be saved. He and his suite were received with great enthusiasm. When de Ruyter, surrounded by the members of the high Council of War, and by

---

15 *Ibid.*, p.328.
16 Jaap Bruijn, *The Dutch Navy of the Seventeenth and Eighteenth Centuries* (Columbia, South Carolina: University of South Carolina Press, 1990), p.99.

the crews that were standing on deck and in the rigging, addressed a few words of
fidelity and devotion to duty to the Prince, praising the brave and threatening the
cowards, enthusiasm rose to fever heat.[17]

The upshot of the discussion was that an attack should now be launched,
both to cover the arrival of the East India fleet and to prevent the landing of
troops.

Rupert, meanwhile, had not waited for a reply to his request for
instructions. His scouts had been watching the Dutch fleet, and on 29 July
reported that it appeared to have left the Schooneveld. Three days later they
reported that de Ruyter was now between Goree and the Maas, and Rupert
convened a council of war on 3 August to discuss the Allied fleet's next
step. It was decided that the fleet should if possible get to the southward
of the enemy, to prevent them regaining their safe anchorage behind the
Schooneveld.[18]

Both fleets were therefore now bent on fighting. De Ruyter, after he
finally left his anchorage, had made his way in heavy weather up the coast,
and anchored some 15 miles south of the Texel. The Allied fleet was at this
time some 30 miles to the north-west of the Texel. For the next few days
the weather steadily deteriorated, effectively preventing movement by either
fleet. Spragge noted in his journal on 7 August that several fireships had been
disabled by the gales; one, the *Golden Hand*, had foundered at anchor. That
day Rupert endeavoured to convene a council of war, but the weather was so
bad that the flag officers were unable to leave their ships.[19]

The storm continued to rage. On the morning of 9 August Spragge ordered
Kempthorne to come to him, but the Vice Admiral was prevented by the
weather. It seems to have abated later on, for Spragge managed to respond to
a signal to come on board Rupert's flagship, which he did 'in very much sea.'
There he learned that the *Papenburg*, a Dutch East Indiaman, had found itself
in the middle of the French squadron, and had been at once taken. It was,
Spragge thought, 'a kind of a little miracle'; the vessel was said to be worth
£100,000. Rupert took the opportunity of his meeting with Spragge to obtain
an assurance that, in his determination to confront Tromp, he would not
become separated from the rest of the fleet.[20]

That day also, Rupert finally received the instructions which he sought.
They were profoundly influenced by diplomatic rather than strategic
considerations; Charles had very much in mind the negotiations going on at
Cologne which might lead to the ending of the war. Anderson summarised
the rather contradictory answer which arrived:

He was not to send for the army before the enemy was 'worsted at sea,' and he
was told that the whole idea of a landing was now 'less advisable than it was at
first.' He was not to attack the Dutch in the Schooneveld. He was not to go further

---

17 Blok, p.341.
18 Anderson, *Third Dutch War*, p.329.
19 *Ibid.*, p.330.
20 Kitson, p.280.

afield than between the Dogger Bank and the Texel in search of the Dutch East Indiamen, 'because it would leave our whole coast exposed, and even the river of Thames, to an enemy sufficiently strong to do a great deal of mischief;' and yet, if necessary he might follow the Indiamen with 'such a number as shall be judged fit for the occasion,' even as far as the Elbe.[21]

The concern not to leave the Thames exposed was not surprising; the events of 1667 in the Medway were a very recent memory.

On the morning of Sunday, 10 August both fleets weighed anchor in what Narbrough described as 'close, hazy weather.' By 8:00 a.m. the Allied fleet was under sail, standing to the south-east; a couple of hours later the Dutch fleet came in sight, heading north. The breeze was now north east by east, 'a fine small gale and the sea smooth.' Narbrough went on to describe the approach to the enemy:

> We steered south east by south, having our two top sails and foresail set. We bore lasking down to the Dutch fleet with our whole fleet, the French squadron leading the van, the General in the middle with the Red Squadron, the Blue Squadron bringing up the rear. All our whole fleet sailing in a line one after each other according to the order of battle prescribed, with the union flag on the mizzen peak of all the Flagships. This forenoon the *Marigold* fire ship was left in the sea dismantled, being ready to sink; I suppose she was defective.[22]

The expression 'lasking down' meant neither by the wind nor before the wind.

Spragge, aboard the *Prince*, was watching carefully to see where Tromp was located in the Dutch line. When de Ruyter, at about 4:00 p.m., tacked, and steered in the same direction as the Allied fleet, it left Tromp in the rear, having all day been leading the Dutch fleet as it approached. Whatever assurance he had given to Rupert, Spragge was still determined to get Tromp, noting in his journal: 'He will, I hope, fall to my share in the Blue Squadron tomorrow, it being now too late to engage.'[23]

The two fleets continued in the same direction until nightfall, although the Dutch, setting more sail, gradually drew ahead. There is a dispute between the English and French accounts of what next occurred. The English version is that Rupert ordered d'Estrées to continue to steer south by east with 'a good sail' until coming into 10 fathoms, and then to turn south between the Dutch and the shore, so as to keep to windward. The French account has it that Rupert's order was that they should go carefully, 'à petite voiles,' because of the risk of shoals, and the accounts of Narbrough and Legge are consistent with this. Anderson therefore concluded that the French version was probably correct. It is important because, as the fleets entered shallower waters the Allied fleet reversed its course; the wind came round to east-south-east, and this put the Dutch to windward. Narbrough was surprised that the Allied fleet should not keep as near the wind as it could, while 'having the

---

21 Anderson, *Third Dutch War*, p.45.
22 *Ibid.*, p.353.
23 *Ibid.*, p.330.

enemy on our lee bow, making sail ahead, as near the wind as they could lie, which was visible to most seamen in our fleet.' He saw that the allies would lose the weather gauge before morning, conceding a crucial advantage to the enemy.[24] Almost certainly, Rupert's caution in shortening sail was because of the shoaling water: by 1:00 a.m. the Red Squadron was sounding 12 fathoms, and Rupert tacked north-north-east. De Ruyter had already gone about, and was well ahead and to windward; and at first light his sails could be seen about 10 miles to the east of the Allied fleet.

There was nothing in the instructions that he had received that prohibited a full scale engagement, and Rupert was determined that, while ensuring that he stayed clear of the shoals, on this occasion there should be a fight.

---

24 Anderson, pp.353-354.

9

The Battle of the Texel

For his part, de Ruyter also had every intention of fighting a pitched battle, in spite of the pronounced inferiority of his fleet. The disparity was, as usual, greater than the mere numbers suggest, because the strength of the individual ships in the Dutch fleet was overall rather less than those in the Allied fleet. The effective odds against him, therefore, were of the order of three to two, but he was used to facing such odds, and was confident of success.

At daybreak on 21 August, when the fleets came in sight of each other, with the wind then being south-easterly, they were roughly to seaward of the Texel channel, with the Dutch to windward. Rupert put the wind at east-south-east, and said that when first sighted the Dutch were 'about a league and a half to windward of us … fair weather and not far from the shore about which time their fleet and ours were standing to the northward.'[1] At that point both fleets were heading north but at about 6:00 a.m. Rupert signalled for the fleet to tack, to follow a course south-west-by-south. This put the French squadron in the van, with Rupert in the centre and Spragge in the rear. De Ruyter followed suit, although electing to wear instead of to tack. Narbrough noted that the fleet 'sailed in very good order in a line, everyone in their station according to the order in the second article in the Fighting Instructions.'[2]

The symmetry with which the two fleets proceeded on their way did not last long. De Ruyter, who had long since grasped the limited extent of the threat offered by the French, had decided to repeat his tactics at Solebay, and mask d'Estrées while concentrating on the English. This time he regarded as sufficient for the purpose to employ only Evertsen's van division of Banckert's squadron. Evertsen closed with Martel, in the French van; d'Estrées with the centre division he left alone, while the rest of Banckert's squadron joined with de Ruyter's squadron in an attack on the French rear division and Rupert's Red Squadron. The effect of this was significantly to shorten the odds faced by de Ruyter, from three to two to four to three.[3]

---

1   *British Naval Documents*, p.219.
2   Anderson, *Third Dutch War*, p.354.
3   *Ibid.*, p.48.

Adriaen Banckert, Vice-Admiral of Zeeland. (Hendrick Berckman, oil on canvas, 1673, Rijkmuseum)

As Anderson points out, naval battles of the time tended to split into three separate actions, squadron against squadron, and on this occasion this was particularly true, because the Allied commanders each had a different view of how the battle should be fought. D'Estrées saw his mission as getting to windward, and not much more; Rupert was prepared for a close action, but wanted to get de Ruyter further out to sea, so that he had more room to manoeuvre; and Spragge did not look beyond his long-running private contest with Tromp. All this, of course, played directly into de Ruyter's hands.

Spragge, in defiance of the assurances he had given to Rupert, deliberately slowed his pace to allow Tromp to come up with the Blue Squadron. Commenting on this later, Rupert sharply observed that the Blue Squadron 'laid their top sails to their masts to stay for them contrary to my express orders and his own duty.'[4] In numbers the two squadrons were closely matched. Spragge had 27 ships, and Tromp 26. Narbrough described the opening of the battle:

The Dutch divisions of ships at that time were got within cannon shot of us; about 8 o'clock they were within fair gun-shot of us; we saluted them with our trumpets and three holloas; presently the Dutch Rear Admiral shot several shot over us and about us; then we fired at him. Thus the fight began, they being to windward of us, and stood to the south westward, as we did.[5]

At about 9:00 a.m., as the battle raged, it began to rain and this continued for some two hours, after which the wind came round to the south. It is not entirely clear what was happening at the head of affairs, where Evertsen was engaging Martel. The latter claimed that he 'was ordered to get the wind and got it,' which was endorsed by the French official account, though others suggested that he failed to weather the enemy. D'Estrées, scarcely engaged, decided that he should 'cut through the Dutch van, so as to get to windward of their whole fleet,' and this he was able to do when Evertsen bore up through the French line to avoid being taken between two fires. Des Ardents's third division followed d'Estrées so that by noon the whole French squadron was to windward, and their immediate opponents were able to support de Ruyter in the centre.

Legge, in the *Royal Katherine*, was immediately ahead of Rupert's *Royal Sovereign*, and was hence in the thick of the battle. He described the situation in his journal:

---

4   *British Naval Documents*, p.219.
5   Anderson, *Third Dutch War*, p.355.

> The wind then being at SW, so that all the French Squadron got the weather gage of the Holland's fleet, but little or no damage to them at all, so that we had all the Holland's fleet to engage with our Red Squadron, only Tromp and his squadron, which did engage Sir Edward Spragge and his squadron. At 12 at noon, de Ruyter and all the Holland's fleet aforesaid being very near his Highness the Prince's stern, we with our ship left our station, which was to be ahead of him, and fell astern between him and the enemy, where we lay battering one at another till three in the afternoon.[6]

Legge recorded the fate of an English fireship which got among the Dutch ships 'thinking to do execution,' but which came under such heavy fire that she was in a sinking condition and all that her crew could do was to set her on fire before abandoning her.

In the rear, the duel between Tromp and Spragge continued unabated. Aboard the *St Michael*, Narbrough noted that her rigging and sails were suffering extensive damage from the Dutch fire: 'Our shrouds and rigging were cut by the enemy shot very much faster than I could get seamen to make it fast again.' At this time he also remarked on a significant feature of the exchange of gunfire, which must have contributed to the way in which the weaker Dutch fleet was able to hold its own: 'The enemy shoot much more shot than we do, and ply their guns faster; they shoot much pound shot, which fly so thick and cut our rigging so much. When the enemy came near us, I could perceive our shot were well placed in them, but when they were at any distance, our shot fell often short.'[7]

Narbrough could see that the *Royal Prince* was also suffering heavy damage. Her mainmast came down, and took the mizzen mast overboard with it, and by 1:00 p.m. she lay there disabled. Spragge sent a message to Ossory to find out his situation; in reply, Ossory said that he would in the *St Michael* stand by the *Royal Prince*. He was as good as his word, fighting off the Dutch vessels that crowded round Spragge's flagship, having seen her disabled. Meanwhile Spragge transferred his flag to the *St George*.

Seeing the blue flag now flying aboard the *St George*, Ossory sent Narbrough over to her to see Spragge, and to ask 'if he would bear down and board the enemy,' in which case he too would board Tromp's flagship. Narbrough made the hazardous journey by boat to the *St George* and delivered Ossory's message to Spragge on the quarterdeck: 'Sir Edward Spragge answered me he would bear down upon the enemy as soon as possible he could, and that he would second my Lord in boarding, and that there would be no great danger in doing it.'[8] Narbrough returned to the *St Michael* and reported, and it was resolved to attempt to board the *Gouden Leeuw*, Tromp's flagship, which was now making sail to get up near the *Royal Prince*. Ossory sent one of his fireships to stand by the dismasted flagship, with orders to attempt to burn any Dutch ship that attacked her. Another fireship, the *Prudent Mary*, headed for the *Gouden Leeuw*, causing Tromp to bear up. The *St Michael* was

---

6   *Ibid.*, p.311.
7   *Ibid.*, p.356.
8   *Ibid.*, p.357.

now to the leeward of the rest of the Blue Squadron; Ossory and Narbrough, seeing that the *St George* was not bearing down to their assistance, 'brought our ship to and handed our sprit sail and kept on our course to the westward along with the *Prince*.'

In the centre the Red Squadron was heavily engaged with de Ruyter's squadron and with the whole of Banckert's squadron except Evertsen's division. De Ruyter had established first a near equality and then, when Evertsen's division came up at 12:30 p.m., a temporary superiority in numbers, and he was determined to take the maximum advantage from this. As a result, Rupert was for the next hour and a half very hard pressed. The wind had come round to the south-west, and some of de Ruyter's ships had got between Rupert and his rear division under Sir John Chicheley, which had been driven to leeward. In his report Rupert set out the position in which he found himself:

> About 12 o'clock I had upon me de Ruyter and his squadron on my lee quarter, an admiral with two flags more on the weather quarter and the Zeeland Squadron upon my broadside to windward. Having fought thus for some time, with both my broadsides to windward and to leeward, I edged down towards the Rear Admiral of the Red forcing the enemy to give way and so joined with them.[9]

By the time that he had completed this manoeuvre, it was after 2:00 p.m., and Rupert was still fighting alone with his squadron, since d'Estrées, who was to windward, made no move to get involved with this action. Rupert was concerned about the fate of the Blue Squadron, which he could see was now about nine miles off to the north-north-east. Not knowing its condition, he decided to take the Red Squadron to its support. As he made sail to do so, de Ruyter followed suit, bearing away with both his squadron and that of Banckert. For the moment, the firing ceased, both sides conserving ammunition, as both Rupert and de Ruyter were running before the wind to reach their rear squadrons. Meanwhile d'Estrées, who of course had not been engaged for some time, was to the southward. He may have been endeavouring to close with Rupert and the Red Squadron, but he was unlikely to be able to catch up the main fleets as they headed north-east.

The fighting between the squadrons of Tromp and Spragge had continued without a pause, with relatively little movement. The order of sailing had left Kempthorne's division at the rear of the Blue Squadron, where he was opposed by the division of Sweers. As the morning progressed the Dutch had been getting the better of this part of the action, and had succeeded in forcing Kempthorne to leeward of the rest of the Blue Squadron. At about 1:00 p.m., though, the Dutch suffered a major blow when Sweers, aboard the *Olifant*, was killed. In the centre, the plan for the *St George* and the *St Michael* to cooperate in a joint boarding attempt on the *Gouden Leeuw* had come to nothing, as Spragge's temporary flagship had been suffering heavy damage and was also now virtually disabled. As a consequence of this,

---

9   *British Naval Documents*, p.220.

Sea battle at Kijkduin (near Texel) on 21 August 1673 between the Dutch fleet under Michiel de Ruyter and Cornelis Tromp and the Anglo-French fleet under Prince Rupert and Count Jean d'Estrées. (Engraving from a contemporary news-sheet, Rijksmuseum)

Spragge decided that he must again shift his flag, and he went aboard a boat to make the transfer. As it lay alongside the crippled *St George*, it was hit by a chance round shot and sank almost once, and Spragge was drowned. Aboard the *St Michael*, Ossory and Narbrough were unable to make out what had happened. It was clear that Spragge's flag had been taken down aboard the *St George*, and Narbrough watched anxiously to see what was going on:

> Some time after, I saw a boat drive astern of the *St George* sunk, and men in the sea swimming about the boat. I saw two boats from our ships to take up the men, and went to the ships again; one was the *St George*'s boat; it was close by the *St George*'s stern. We ever looking when the Blue flag would be put up on some of our ships which were near the *St George* at the time.[10]

The *St Michael* herself was now getting into a bad state; the damage to her sails and rigging was now so extensive that it was becoming impossible to work the ship. Both her top sails had been shot to pieces, and her yards were smashed, while the mizzen top mast had gone by the board. It was impossible to set the mainsail, mizzen or staysails, and the best she could do was to keep on with her foresail, while endeavouring to shield the *Royal Prince* and get her away from the enemy. The Dutch, too, had been suffering; the damage to the *Gouden Leeuw* had become so serious that Tromp, too, was obliged to

---

10   Anderson, *Third Dutch War*, p.358.

shift his flag to the *Komeetster* when his flagship began to fall behind the rest of his squadron.

Meanwhile Rupert and de Ruyter had been making progress towards their embattled rear squadrons. Narbrough spotted what he described as 'a great fleet of warships' to the south-west, and assumed that these were the Red and White Squadrons coming to rejoin the Blue Squadron. He then realised that the newcomers were in two groups, and as they approached saw that the nearer had Dutch flags and colours, while the other was English. What was striking as these two fleets advanced was that neither was firing at the other. The Dutch force was further to the east than the English, and Tromp made sail to leeward of the *Royal Prince*; he and the rest of his squadron stood to the eastward, and as they weathered her they engaged in a brisk exchange with the divisions of Kempthorne and Ossory.

Behind Tromp came two Dutch fireships which attempted to lay the *Royal Prince* on board. They faced intense fire, however from both the *St Michael* and the *Royal Prince* herself, and were unable to grapple with her. Having been set on fire before they were able to do so, they drifted, burning, away from their target. Ossory despatched Captain Griffith of the *Hampshire* to take the *Royal Prince* in tow, while Narbrough did his best to get enough sails hoisted to enable the *St Michael* to follow Tromp in order to resume the action.

Seeing no blue flag on any of the squadron, and no ship behaving as if Spragge were aboard, Narbrough realised that he must have been killed. He could see the *Royal Charles*, which formed part of Spragge's division, moving rapidly ahead 'as if she had been bound away with an express from us'; in fact her captain had been mortally wounded. Narbrough could see Tromp's squadron now some way astern, and that they were engaged in repairing their rigging, while de Ruyter was approaching, evidently with the intention of preventing the Blue Squadron from joining Rupert. This manoeuvre failed; when Rupert and the Red Squadron arrived, Narbrough noted the signal flying aboard the flagship:

> Our General having the blue flag at his mizzen peak, a sign for all ships to windward of him to bear down into his wake and grain, the French squadron and some of our ships of the Red Squadron kept to windward and would not bear down according to the signal given by our General. We kept the wind what we could, to get into our General's wake.[11]

The reference to 'grain' means a position ahead of a ship, as 'wake' is astern.

It had taken Rupert a considerable time to reach the Blue Squadron. By his reckoning he came near by around 4:00 p.m.; Narbrough put it at about 5:00 p.m., while Legge thought it as late as 6:00 p.m. Narbrough is generally the most accurate reporter of the events around him, and it may be taken that it was at about 5:00 when Rupert flew his signal for the fleet to take station on the *Royal Sovereign*. This marked the end of the independent battle between Tromp and the Blue Squadron. Narbrough claimed that the English had had

---

11 *Ibid.*, p.360.

The *Royal Charles*. Launched as the *Naseby*, this was the ship that brought the returning King, Charles II, back to England. It was classed as an 80-gun first rate ship of the line. Larger than the *Sovereign*, it was the first three-deck ship in the Navy. It fought at Lowestoft, the Four Days' Battle and St James' Day Battle. It was captured in the raid on the Medway and sold for scrap in 1673. (Pen and ink drawing by Abraham Stork, 1672, open source)

the best of it: 'In case de Ruyter and his fleet had not come to leeward of us, we had destroyed Tromp and his squadron before night; Tromp was standing clear away, had he not seen the Dutch fleet come towards us.'[12] On the other hand, Dutch accounts suggest that the Blue Squadron would certainly have been overwhelmed had not Rupert arrived in support. Anderson concludes that in truth the two sides had more or less fought themselves to a standstill, and were doing their best to refit and make good damage when their respective commanders-in-chief arrived on the scene. Rupert's report, though, does rather suggest that the Dutch claim was not without merit; after recording his signal for the fleet to concentrate, he went on:

> Whereupon we bore up and steered in between de Ruyter and our lame ships, and fired guns to some of our own ships to windward to bear down, but none of them came near to assist me, except Sir John Kempthorne and my Lord of Ossory so that I had great reason to believe that except I had come in so happily to their relief the Blue Squadron had been totally lost since they were so disabled as no more of them but those two flags only did give me any assistance after I came down.[13]

The battle was far from over. Rupert, though, was able to collect only 11 or 12 ships of the line with which to renew the fighting. Among them were the flagships of Kempthorne, Ossory and Harman, together with the *Triumph* (Davies), *Warspite* (Stout), Sir John Holmes (*Rupert*), Legge, in the *Royal Katherine*, *Resolution* (Sir John Berry) *Henry* (Sir John Emly), *Mary* (Sir Roger Strickland) and *Crown* (Carter). The fight, Rupert reported, 'was very sharp and close.' In the course of it he sent in two fireships, which he claimed increased the disorder into which he had forced de Ruyter's fleet.

---

12 *Ibid.*
13 *British Naval Documents*, p.221.

Narbrough's account of the fireships, which at that time had the weather gauge, describes how they were set on fire before coming at the enemy: 'These fireships put the Dutch fleet in great disorder; they ran up in a huddle to get clear of the fire, which disorder in the Dutch gave our fleet a great advantage, our fleet being to windward of the Dutch, but did not make use of it.'[14]

Rupert's description of this phase of the battle as having been 'sharp and close' was born out by Legge's account in his journal, in which he wrote: 'Then from 6 to 8 at night we were very smartly engaged, our masts, yards, rigging and sails much disabled and several men slain and wounded.'[15]

It was during this period that occurred the incident which was to lead to the very greatest controversy. Although there was no doubt that he had seen Rupert's signal of a blue flag at the mizzen, d'Estrées failed to close up and attack the enemy's rear, although he was to windward and perfectly able to comply with the order. Martel, who also saw the signal and understood its meaning, expected d'Estrées to obey, and was disgusted at his failure to do so. The French admiral disingenuously sent a messenger to Rupert's flagship to enquire the meaning of the signal, but neither in the immediate aftermath of the battle or later has much credence been attached to his professed ignorance.

As night began to fall, the battle came to an end. The Allied fleet continued on a north-westerly course, while de Ruyter turned eastward, satisfied that he had done enough. Rupert watched him go with considerable relief:

> The enemy, when dark night came, stood off to their own coast, which I had reason to be glad of, resolving if I could avoid it not to venture a new engagement the next day, unless I could have had a better assurance not only what the Count d'Estrées but many of my own meant to do who had failed me so in this. In this battle neither English nor French lost one ship of war, neither do I think the Dutch have great reason to rejoice, and considering all things, I think it the greatest Providence ever befell me in my life that I brought off his Majesty's fleet so.[16]

The fire-eating Narbrough did not share Rupert's satisfaction at the ending of the battle:

> Thus the enemy and our fleet parted: we having the weather gage of the enemy, stood away from them, a sight unpleasant to the English seamen. I hope never to see nor to hear of the like again. I had rather fall in the battle than ever to see the like more, that so mighty a fleet of ships as ours is to stand away, as now we do, from so mean a fleet as the Dutch fleet is to ours, without the loss of one ship or any other damage considerable to us.[17]

In spite of the expenditure of a huge amount of ammunition in the course of a battle that had lasted a whole day, casualties were again surprisingly low

---

14 Anderson, *Third Dutch War*, p.361.
15 *Ibid.*, p.311.
16 *British Naval Documents*, pp.221–222.
17 Anderson, *Third Dutch War*, p.361.

Encounter during the Battle of Kijkduin. (Willem van de Velde (II), oil on canvas, 1675, Rijksmuseum)

in both ships and men. As Rupert had noted, no Allied ship had been sunk, and no Dutch ship either, apart from fire ships. Five English ships (*Royal Prince*, *Gloucester*, *Advice*, *Stavoren* and *Portsmouth*) had been disabled and were at once sent home for repairs, and four Dutch ships (*Gouden Leeuw*, *Hollandia*, *Voorsichtigheid* and *Provincie van Utrecht*) likewise. As usual, though, there had been a considerable number of high profile casualties. In addition to Spragge, five captains in the Allied fleet died; the most notable of these was Rupert's long-standing friend Sir William Reeves, First Captain of the *Royal Sovereign*. The others were le Neve of the *Edgar*, Hayward of the *Royal Charles*, Courtney of the *Dunkirk* and d'Estival of the French *Invincible*. Apart from Sweers, the Dutch also lost Jan de Liefde, de Ruyter's son-in-law van Gelder of the *Steenburgen*, Sweerius (or Sweers) of the *Beschermer*, Visscher of the *Wapen van Medemblik* and Kiela of the *Ter Veere*. The total number of casualties on each side is very uncertain. A Dutch source gives the losses of the Amsterdam squadron, which made up more than a third of the fleet, as 71 killed and 120 wounded, with the rest in proportion. A list published in 1801 records the losses of the Blue Squadron as being 138 killed and 278 wounded. According to Narbrough the *St Michael* lost 52 men killed and 71 wounded. His first suggestion was that the total of English casualties was less than 500, but this may have referred only to those killed; the *Royal Sovereign* lost 60 killed or dangerously wounded. The only figure for French losses is for *La Reine*, amounting to 30 killed or wounded.[18]

On each side fresh appointments were required of flag officers. Spragge's place was taken by Sir John Harman, hitherto Vice Admiral of the Red; he was succeeded by Ossory. Sir John Holmes became Rear Admiral of the Red. Surprisingly, a flag appointment was not found for Narbrough, who before

---

18 *Ibid.*, pp.52–53.

the campaign began had been designated as Rear Admiral of the Red, but who had not returned in time to take up the post. For the Dutch, de Haen and Jan Van Nes were promoted to the posts held by Sweers and de Liefde, their places being taken by de Ruyter's son Engel and by Cornelis de Liefde, though this last appointment was for some reason not confirmed by the Prince of Orange.[19]

On 23 August Rupert convened a council of war, the fleet then being anchored some 50 or 60 miles west of Vlieland. The decision made was for the Allies to appear off Scheveningen, as much to show the flag and demonstrate that the Dutch had not defeated them as any strategic consideration. Storms, however, prevented this, and in any case provisions were running low. Rupert went to Yarmouth to refit, intending as soon as possible to return to the Dutch coast, suggesting that 'the French are ashamed of the part they played and will retrieve their honour.' That may have been the message he got from Martel, who sent him an apologetic memorandum, but there is no reason to suppose that d'Estrées would have reconsidered the way in which he would conduct his squadron. As the days went by, delays in reprovisioning the fleet, coupled with adverse weather, prevented Rupert from carrying out his intention. The campaigning season was coming to an end, and on 10 September the French began preparations to return to Brest, although prevailing conditions prevented this until November. De Ruyter had meanwhile been ordered to sail to the English coast to make a nuisance of himself, and by doing so to claim the victory, but in his turn he was frustrated by bad weather, and returned home; by mid September the various contingents of his fleet had returned to their home ports.

As with many naval battles, that at the Texel had been, in the narrowest sense, indecisive, but looked at in its strategic context it had been another victory for de Ruyter; the Allied fleet had been sufficiently damaged to ensure that no invasion was possible, and the valuable Dutch trading fleets were safe. One English historian, Colonel Rogers, suggests that one of the factors leading to the Allied failure to defeat the Dutch, in addition to the ability of de Ruyter and the treachery of Louis XIV and d'Estrées, was the incompetence of Prince Rupert.[20] It is a charge that is not sustained by the facts. Given the overall circumstances in which the battle was fought, there was not much more that Rupert could possibly have done.

Other historians have not failed to recognise that the battle had indeed ended in a Dutch victory. Mahan quoted with approval the verdict of the English naval historian Campbell, in *Lives of the Admirals*:

> The consequences which the Dutch, through the prudence of their Admiral, drew from this battle were exceedingly great; for they opened their ports, which were entirely blocked up, and put an end to all thoughts, by removing the possibility, of an invasion.[21]

---

19 *Ibid.*, p.53.
20 Colonel H.C.B. Rogers, *Generals-at-Sea* (Bromley: Galago, 1992), p.153.
21 Mahan, p.154.

10

Conclusion

While Michiel de Ruyter was successfully protecting the coasts of the United Provinces from the might of the Allied fleet, ensuring that no invasion could take place, a small Dutch squadron was causing havoc among the English possessions on the other side of the Atlantic. The exploits of the squadron led by Cornelius Evertsen the Youngest have been recounted in detail by the American historians Donald G. Shomette and Robert D. Haslach, and demonstrate just what could be achieved against the remote and ill-defended colonies of Central and North America by a small, well led and determined force.

The project had its inception in the Dutch plan to intercept a valuable English East India fleet which was due to arrive at St Helena in the autumn of 1672. Evertsen was to take a small squadron to the South Atlantic. His flagship was the 48-gun *Swanenburgh*, formerly the English *St Patrick*, which had been captured in 1667. The squadron, which also included two other former English vessels, now named *Schaeckerloo* and *Suriname*, and two smaller vessels, put to sea on 5 December, and slipped through the Channel, reaching the Canary Islands in January 1673.[1]

Evertsen went on to the Cape Verde Islands. There, in February, he encountered an English squadron under Captain Richard Munden, whose mission was also to proceed to St Helena, with the object of capturing a Dutch East India fleet that was also expected in the vicinity. It was apparent to Evertsen that the English squadron was considerably stronger than his own, and it seemed to him pointless to attempt to carry out his primary mission. Accordingly, he abandoned his St Helena objective, and proceeded to undertake what had been designated as his next mission. This was to go to Surinam, to defend the Dutch colony there, or, if it had been captured, to retake it.

After dealing with the situation in Surinam, Evertsen's instructions allowed him to raid northwards to Virginia and the territories formerly

---

1   Shomette and Haslach, p.59.

known as the New Netherlands. Should the attempt at St Helena fail, he was to 'attack, to ransack or even occupy' Bermuda. In addition:

> A cruise shall be undertaken before and along the coasts of Virginia, New Netherland, without forgetting New Found Land, subsequently capturing and ruining there whatever shall be possible so that, should the design against the island of St Helena have miscarried, which is not surmised, to acquire through this [cruise] so much booty, that the expenses of this equipment shall be generously defrayed through the same.[2]

Before leaving the Caribbean, however, Evertsen attempted a move against Martinique. This was more strongly defended than he had expected, and he abandoned the enterprise, and pressed on northwards, now in company with another Dutch squadron operating in the area under the command of Jacob Benckes. Their next call was at Montserrat, followed by a skirmish at Nevis. One of Evertsen's principal tasks was, of course, to take prizes wherever he could, and in this he enjoyed considerable success. On 29 May the combined squadron took St Eustatius and held it temporarily before moving north to Puerto Rico.[3]

In Virginia the governor, William Berkeley, was aware that a Dutch squadron was on the loose, and he took defensive measures. In particular he was able to call on an English squadron commanded by Captains Gardiner and Cotterell, which had been strengthened by the addition of a number of armed merchantmen. On 10 July Evertsen and Benckes approached Chesapeake Bay. Two days later they engaged the English squadron in a brisk encounter, which was, however, indecisive. Thereafter the Dutch picked up a number of prizes before withdrawing, and then headed north to New York.

In 1673 the city had been an English possession for only six years, its name changed from New Amsterdam. Located at the southern tip of Manhattan Island, it consisted of only about 300 buildings, and had a population of about 2,500, who were mainly Dutch. The city was defended by Fort James, which was not particularly strong. The Dutch arrived off Sandy Hook on 29 July. Evertsen and Benckes convened a council of war which resolved on an immediate attack. Next day a force of 600 Marines and seamen went ashore, and Fort James soon capitulated after only a brief resistance. In the following days the ineffectual Governor Lovelace was taken prisoner.

On 8 August Evertsen and Benckes despatched a squadron under Captain Nicholas Boes with a mission to attack the Newfoundland fishing fleet and to break up its infrastructure. Thereafter Boes was to proceed to Fayal in the Azores, and await the arrival there of the rest of the squadron. Meanwhile the Dutch proceeded to re-establish their rule in the colony of New Orange, as the former New Netherlands was now named. Evertsen and Benckes had no intention of remaining, although the Dutch population, amounting to about 6,000 in all, pressed them to stay to defend the colony against the inevitable English counter-attacks. The danger was not immediate: the neighbouring

---

2   *Ibid.*, p.74.
3   *Ibid.*, p.115.

English colony of Connecticut effectively offered to remain neutral if the Dutch left them alone.[4]

A tiny force under Captain Anthony Colve, the commander of the *Swanenburgh*'s marines, was left to uphold Dutch rule, and as autumn approached Evertsen and Benckes set sail for their rendezvous with Boes in the Azores. The squadron was reunited there by October. Boes had carried out his mission to Newfoundland with considerable effect. He had arrived first at Ferryland, where he plundered and systematically destroyed everything in sight. He went on to St John's, where he encountered greater resistance, so moved on to attack the fishing fleet itself. He destroyed some 150 vessels, taking eight as prizes, before setting off to the Azores.

While there the combined squadron, with its numerous prizes, was hit by a storm of extreme violence. This was so severe that several prizes were lost as the tempest raged. Once it subsided, Evertsen had to decide what he should now do, and after three weeks he resolved to make for Cadiz. The plan was, when the Dutch arrived there, to prey on richly laden English merchant vessels in and about the Straits of Gibraltar, but in this venture they enjoyed no success, and returned homeward, successfully evading English warships in the channel.

Back in America, the expected English counter-attacks had begun. An offensive launched from Maryland retook Hoerner Kill, which had been occupied by the Dutch in September, while Colve faced immediate threats from a force collected in Connecticut. Back home, the Dutch authorities had been amazed and delighted by the extent of the successes that had been achieved in America, but were far from clear as to what could be done to hold on to the newly recovered territories. In practice, there was really nothing that could be done; and it is unsurprising that in the subsequent peace negotiations that ultimately led to the Treaty of Westminster in 1674, it was agreed that each side should retain what they possessed before the war broke out. Nevertheless Evertsen and Benckes had achieved remarkable success with very limited resources.

By the autumn of 1673 Charles II was in a very bad place. De Ruyter's success in resisting the Allied fleet; the popular disapproval of the French alliance exacerbated by the apparent French treachery at sea and by energetic Dutch inspired lobbying of public opinion; the evident intention of Louis XIV to involve England in his war against Spain – all these put intense pressure on the King. But above all it was the absolute necessity to raise money for the continuation of the war that left him entirely vulnerable to Parliament. There was no prospect of any further subsidy from the French, and Osborne, the Lord Treasurer, had made it abundantly clear that there was, quite simply, no money to finance further operations in 1674. There had been, it is true, the windfall gains from the capture of three Dutch East India ships at St Helena by the squadron which Evertsen had encountered, together with that taken by the Allied fleet in 1673. The King's more hawkish advisers argued that these gains, valued together at £300,000, could be used to finance at least

---

4   *Ibid.*, p.190.

some limited naval operations next year. However, they were entirely offset by the heavy and damaging losses suffered as a result of Evertsen's successful raid on the Americas.[5]

Charles cannot have approached the next meeting of Parliament, therefore, with a great deal of confidence, but he did his best. Parliament met on 27 October, against a background of the deeply rooted anti-papist prejudices of the people, which fuelled a profound suspicion of royal motivation. Asking for 'speedy supply', the King put the best face he could on his request, arguing that the safety and honour of the nation required it. He and his supporters put forward the case that continuation of the war was essential for the protection of English trade, but this cut little ice with those members of Parliament who identified themselves with public opinion. Opposition to the King was led by Sir William Coventry, who once again proved himself a skilful Parliamentary tactician. In his first speech he denounced the French alliance, and the proven faithlessness of Louis XIV, pointing in particular to the alleged French treachery at the battle of the Texel. His withering attack culminated in a succinct analysis of the true position: 'The interest of the King of England is to keep France from being too great on the Continent, and the French interest is to keep us from being masters of the sea – the French have pursued that interest well.'[6] He followed this with a thunderous attack on the proposition that the war would enhance English trade or bring increased profits or wealth.

Coventry understood that even if there was a majority in the House of Commons simply to reject the request for supply, it would have the effect of putting Parliament in the position of responsibility for any military or naval defeat, and for a disadvantageous peace. Instead, therefore, he put forward a resolution that the Commons would not consider voting the requested supply unless it was shown that 'the obstinacy of the Dutch made it necessary to continue the war, and unless the kingdom had been secured from the dangers of popery.'[7] Since Charles could not resist this outright, he prorogued Parliament in the hope that he could assemble sufficient support before it returned. When it did so on 7 January, he argued that only by it voting supply could a 'good fleet' enable a 'good peace.' The King did not create a convincing impression, lying through his teeth in denying the existence of a secret treaty with Louis. Further parliamentary manoeuvring did him no good. Professor Jones finds a particularly ironic and symbolic significance in the fact that Sir George Downing, whose virulently anti-Dutch feelings had been central to the outbreak of war, now spoke for peace.

This was finally concluded by the Treaty of Westminster on 19 February 1674. Charles had little to show for the war that he had gone out of his way to cause. The Dutch agreed to salute the English flag as a matter of courtesy, but did not concede English sovereignty of the sea. The overseas conquests made reverted to their previous owners, so Surinam remained Dutch and New York English. No concession was made by the Dutch in respect of their right

---

5　Jones, p.216.
6　*Ibid.*, p.214.
7　*Ibid.*, p.215.

to fish in the North Sea. Jones trenchantly summed up the war, writing that 'the third war was a bogus affair from its aggressive start to its whimpering end.' Charles deserved to fail, and fail he did; those who lost their lives did so to no decent purpose. And, of course, the dishonesty of the English King was matched by that of the French.

No one will ever know exactly what instructions Louis XIV actually gave to d'Estrées, but the consensus among historians is that the French admiral's proceedings strongly indicate that he was to avoid engaging the Dutch too closely. Orders to this effect would override whatever Rupert instructed d'Estrées to do, and the existence of such an injunction is the most probable explanation for his failure to carry out Rupert's orders.

Rupert was the most vociferous contemporary critic of the conduct of the French. In his report of the battle he was in no doubt of the consequences of d'Estrées's disobedience at the crucial time:

> If the French then lying within distance to windward had obeyed my signal and borne down upon the enemy according to their duty, I must have routed and torn them all to pieces; it was the plainest and greatest opportunity was ever lost at sea … When came a message from Count d'Estrées to receive orders and know the meaning of the blue flags being on the mizzen peak, which I wondered at since there was no instruction plainer to be understood or more necessary among the general instructions for fighting which he had laid before him and besides it wanted neither signal nor instruction to tell him what he should then have done, the case was so plain to every man's eye in the whole fleet.[8]

Rupert's first reaction had not been to put all the blame for the disappointing outcome of the battle on the French. He was extremely critical of Spragge for the way in which he chose to fight a separate battle with Tromp. At a meeting with d'Estrées on the day after the battle, the French commander explained that he had not understood what Rupert wanted and did not know the meeting of the crucial signal. At this stage Rupert was uncertain whether the wind would have enabled the French to give the required support. And he understood the consequence of a public dispute with an ally: the King in a letter of 20 August asked him to suppress criticism of the French as far as possible 'lest the enemy come to gain a greater advantage upon us than they can possibly gain by fighting.'[9] Charles was only too well aware of the effect on English public opinion of official complaints about the French.

It did not take long for Rupert to make up his mind where the blame lay. He had written to the King on 17 August to tell him that it was not only the English who complained about d'Estrées: 'I must as my duty binds me acquaint you that both officers and marines of the French are extremely unsatisfied with their generals not bearing in … more than your Majesty can imagine.'[10] There was already a great deal of public discussion about the conduct of the French. One Dutch seaman is said to have commented in the

---

8   *British Naval Documents*, p.221.
9   Kitson, p.288.
10 *Ibid.*

course of a discussion as to why the French did not come down: 'You fools! They have had the English to fight for them, and all their business here is to see that they earn their wages.'[11]

The case for d'Estrées was put forward by a number of his captains, and for a while these carried some weight. It was claimed that the French failure to get into action was due to the lightness of the wind, and also that the swell was so heavy that they would not have been able to open their gun ports to use their lower batteries.[12] There were thus three quite separate explanations on offer, none of which carried much conviction, and they were all blown away by the intervention of the Marquis de Martel, the commander of the French van. On 27 August he wrote a long letter to Colbert with a detailed account of the battle, explaining that d'Estrées had ordered that no attack should be made by the French without direct written or oral instructions from him. He observed that 'd'Estrées has dishonoured the nation having done everything as badly as possible. The English have good reason not to be satisfied with him.'[13]

Martel was so angry that he went on to publish a pamphlet, in which he stated that, on seeing Rupert's signal:

> He laid his sails to the masts expecting that Mons. d'Estrées would advance with his whole squadron and fall altogether with this fair wind upon the body of the enemy and send in fireships among them; but instead of that he kept the wind and contented himself to give his ships leave to shoot at more than [a] cannon and [a] half distance from the enemy. Mons. de Martel saw very well how shameful this was.[14]

For his pains Martel was sent by Louis XIV to the Bastille. In England, the effect of his disclosures was to confirm the public's darkest suspicions about the French.

Louis ordered an inquiry by de Seuil, the intendant of the Navy at Brest; Mahan concluded that this left 'little doubt of the dishonour of the French arms in this battle.' He went on to quote Troude, a French naval historian, who wrote:

> M. d'Estrées gave it to be understood that the King wished his fleet spared, and that the English should not be trusted. Was he wrong in not relying upon the sincerity of the English alliance, when he was receiving from all quarters warnings that the people and the nobles were murmuring against it, and Charles II was perhaps alone in his kingdom in wishing it?[15]

Mahan added a quotation from de Seuil's official report: 'it would appear in all these sea fights Ruyter has never cared to attack the French squadron, and

---

11 Mahan, p.155.
12 Jenkins, p.54.
13 Kitson, p.288.
14 Spencer, p.358.
15 Quoted in Mahan, p.155.

that in this last action he had detached ten ships of the Zeeland squadron to keep it in play.' This, Mahan considered, was the clearest evidence of de Ruyter's opinion of 'the inefficiency or faithlessness of that contingent of the Allied forces.'[16]

In the course of de Seuil's inquiry d'Estrées had really let the cat out of the bag when he spoke of the French King's wish that his ships be 'husbanded'. He also offered a complaint that Martel had failed to support him, but 'courut un grand bord à la mer.' To this, Martel replied that he was repairing damage, an explanation which d'Estrées offered for his own failure to follow up the enemy. He also claimed that Rupert and de Ruyter, heavily engaged, 'had been steering so far off the wind that they were almost out of reach.' Anderson observed that in any case he ought to have been able to join in the fighting between the centre squadrons very nearly as soon as Banckert and Evertsen.[17] He also observed that even French historians conceded that the French fleet could and should have done more, but that their views as to the reason for this differed widely:

> Sue has no doubt whatever that d'Estrées had secret orders from Louis XIV not to risk his ships for the sake of the English. Jal, on the other hand, ridicules this suggestion and concludes that d'Estrées acted as he did ' not in accordance with alleged secret orders from the King, but out of pure vanity, and because he was never willing to consult anyone or to listen to anyone's advice.'[18]

Looking at d'Estrées's conduct of the French squadron throughout the war, and his varied and conflicting excuses for his diffidence during the battle of the Texel, as well as his candid observations to de Seuil about the King's wish to 'husband' his fleet, it seems overwhelmingly probable that Louis did indeed give him secret instructions. The consequence of the battle had, it has been suggested, long-term effects on English willingness to trust foreign allies: 'With a sturdy commonsense the English people henceforward determined to be at the mercy of no ally, whose conduct at a critical moment might be governed by his own interests, prejudices or policies: the unhappy history of the fate of treaties, of guarantees and the like, affords ample evidence of the wisdom of that decision.'[19]

The diffidence with which d'Estrées handled his fleet did of course materially reduce the effect of the numerical disadvantage which de Ruyter faced at the Texel, but this detracted little from the extent of his achievement there, and in the preceding battles of the war. Throughout, he had been the outstanding commander, and showed once again why he is entitled to be regarded as one of the great admirals in naval history. Again and again he showed that he was much more than a match for the enemy commanders which he faced. Rupert and James were both competent leaders, though each

---

16 Mahan, pp.155–156.
17 Anderson, *Third Dutch War*, p.49.
18 *Ibid.*, p.55.
19 Richmond, p.187.

had his own faults, but neither possessed the qualities necessary to make numbers tell against de Ruyter.

His strategic situation necessitated his fighting a defensive campaign, and to do so with fewer ships than his opponents, and which in general were of lesser fighting power. Because of this, he was obliged to choose with care the occasions on which to fight. His primary function was to protect the Dutch coasts from invasion; a secondary, but important consideration was to ensure that the rich Dutch East India fleets came safely home. He was entirely successful in achieving both these objectives.

He overcame the difficulties inherent in the Dutch system of naval administration, as he did also the political unrest which seemed almost as if it would engulf him personally. He loyally carried out the instructions given him, but he did not let these get in the way of his brilliant opportunism. Of this, the supreme example was when he surprised the Allied fleet at Solebay; but for the failure of the wind at the critical moment, his victory would have been much more emphatic.

Throughout his career de Ruyter was always prudent in the decisions which he took, looking ahead to calculate the possible consequences, but this did not prevent him being an inspirational leader. His subordinates trusted, with good reason, his tactical insight. Willing to take risks when the occasion demanded it, he kept his eye firmly on the overall strategic situation. Abraham van der Moer, in his essay on de Ruyter in *The Great Admirals*, published in 1997, observed: 'A master in distinguishing between matters of major and minor importance, he never lost sight of the ultimate aim and always put the most important things first.'[20]

De Ruyter stands, therefore, as one of the great figures of European history. Remarkably, he was also an admirable human being, as van der Moer observes; no one has ever sought to tarnish his reputation, and no one would succeed if he did: 'Upon becoming acquainted with the life of Michiel Adriaenszoon de Ruyter, one has to pass through a period of mild disbelief. The picture that emerges is almost too perfect. Yet the facts are incontestable.'[21] No wonder, therefore, that one biography should end with words that perhaps seem extravagant, but which in the context of the times may perhaps be considered justifiable:

> He was not only a model of pure patriotism, of devotion to duty, of unflinching courage, an incomparably balanced mixture of audacity and prudence, a perfect hero, a great sailor, and a born leader in battle. He was also a noble man, a character without blemish, honest and direct, faithful and just, upon whom everybody, low or exalted, could rely implicitly. He was simple, humble, pious as well as frank, and all those who knew him praise him as a model father not only to his own family but to the men of the fleets he commanded.[22]

---

20 A. van der Moer, 'Michiel Adriaenszoon de Ruyter' in *The Great Admirals*, ed. Jack Sweetman (Annapolis, MD: Naval Institute Press, 1997), p.89.

21 *Ibid.*

22 Blok, p.388.

Appendix I

Minutes of the Privy Council Committee on Foreign Affairs, Whitehall, 18 April 1672

[Present:] the King, Royal Highness [Duke of York], Lord Arlington, Prince Rupert, Mr Treasurer [Shaftesbury], Earl Lauderdale, Navy [Board]

[added in margin: the Navy [Board] Officers attending: Sir R Holmes, Earl Sandwich]

1. If the ships be ready and the Dutch not out they go into the Downs.
2. Question whether they go westward immediately or rather not unless the Dutch come upon them.

Earl Sandwich. Not unless the Dutch press them. But to stay there to await if the Dutch come into the River, then to fall in behind them

The K[ing]. If they go not till they press them, their small frigates will certainly get up with the worst sailors of ours, and so by consequence engage the whole fleet.

NB Ours in this case must haul in, and having not the windfall necessarily the fleet will be engaged. They will certainly harry the ships the stern most ships, and so either she is lost, or else the whole fleet must engage.

Pr[ince] R[upert]. They will never so engage any of ours if they see us get between these light frigates and cut them off.

D[uke of] Y[ork]. You may put them if carried into Rye H[arbour].

Pr[ince] R[upert]. They will not tack upon you, if you be 50 ships.

Earl Lauderdale. If you get them down as low as Beachy, with word [illegible] fall upon them and destroy them.

The K[ing]. They will not press you into the Channel, for fear of the Fr[ench] K[ing]. Therefore

2. Upon the whole, stay in the Downs to the French come up, to be then at liberty what to do as they see reasonable on the place.

[Prince] Ru[pert]. If they come and lie in the Gunfleet now before you be out, what then? Whether to stay for the French, or attack them ourselves.

3. Duke York. Pr[ince] R[upert] to attack them so soon as the French are heard off the Isle of Wight. For the Dutch will not fight in the sands but edge out into the sea, and then shall ever have room to pass by them into the Downs and so to the French and lose them in the night etc.

4. Ru[pert]. Notwithstanding the French will the Dutch be actually before you in the River, and then will the Dutch nakedly etc.

The English pilots in the French fleet, if maimed, shall have the same allowance as ours have.

The [illegible] frigate at Newcastle to be sent to bring all colliers they can.

Minutes of the privy Council committee on foreign affairs, 2 May 1672

The fleet

When we are joined with the French what then to do?

Res[olved] Not in the Downs no safety etc. Off of Dungeness, that's the safest. Not to fight them so as that being beat they may get into their ports, and to boat out again upon us.

Pr[ince Robert] [Rupert] you will find if you go to Dungeness, the Dutch will go northwards to Tynemouth and stop the colliers go[ing]. If at Dungeness, you find them do so, find them out wherever they are, lest you dishearten your men.

The K[ing]. Dungeness is dangerous for S. and S. by E. [winds] for the great ships.

Pr[ince] R[upert]. No, a south wind carries you directly into the Downs.

Mr Tr[easurer]. Stay in the Downs till all the ships are nigher. Then be the Dutch where they will go, and waylay their trade on the Dogger Bank. And there you catch all they have abroad. There you rather fight them and with advantage of place or interrupt their trade.

Pr[ince] R[upert]. If you fight so with them as to be between them and Holland, and fight and happen to lose the day, all is lost, for the fleet will be lost …

The Pr[ince]. Lie at the Wash till you see what the Dutch does. If they force you to fight by annoying the country, fight them. If not, drive them on etc.

The King. Why not the Duke [of York] come down to St Helens to ripen the French in passage and Rules of sailing and fighting etc. before they fall in with the Dutch.

The Pr[ince]. Do we keep the French too long at sea without fighting?

The King. By no means.

Lord Arlington. Fears the F[rench] will not come into the Channel till they hear the K[ing']s fleet is actually in the [four words illegible] of the D[uke] gets in the Downs, away with two expresses one by land, one by sea, with all speed. Res[olved]

The King. The Duke to have all these perils listed to him, but to leave the resolution of them to him upon the place, Give the D[uke of York] no absolute orders either to lie at the Downs, at Dungeness, or – – – – – – – – – [sic], but leave all to be resolved by him, as they shall think best.

That by land to go through France. That by sea, to go to Plymouth with orders to the governor to press a vessel etc.

D[uke of] Laud[erdale]. Suppose when the Duke [of York] is in the Downs or at Dungeness before the French fleet arrives, what is then to do by an east wind etc.?

The King. They will never venture into the Channel to fight us fearing it a trap, with an easterly wind all things would be lost.

Res[olved]. Or[der]s not to lie in Downs by any means.

Res[olved]. of the p[erils] of the station to be offered to the Duke and left to him to be resolved.

The King. Every ship has three suits of sails and all rigging prepared with seven cables in every ship.

Only small rigging, if wanting must be examined what store we have, if not, then in town bespeak them, especially shrouds.

Pr[ince] R[upert]. This service will not be done, unless you have here the shrouds etc. and small rigging in one secure great [gratt] store house or magazine.

Have all these ready at Chatham as the best place. The Pr[ince] and G[ene]ral repaired all thing there. [Probably a reference to the Duke of Monmouth, Captain-General, 1670–9][1]

---

1   *British Naval Documents*, pp.196–198.

Appendix II

The Fleets at Solebay

The Allied Fleet

White Squadron		Red Squadron		Blue Squadron	
Terrible (Duquesne, R.Ad.)	70	London (Spragge, V.Ad.)	96	St Andrew (Kempthorne, R.Ad.)	96
Illustre	70	Old James	70	French Ruby	80
Conquérant	70	Resolution	70	St George	70
Admirable	68	Dunkirk	60	Warspite	70
Téméraire	50	Monk	60	Gloucester	62
Prince	50	Bristol	48	Bonaventure	48
Bourbon	50	Diamond	48	Antelope	48
Vaillant	50	Sweepstakes	36		
Alcion	46	Dartmouth	32		
Hasardeux	38				
Saint Philippe (d'Estrées, V.Ad.)	78	Prince (Duke of York, Ad.)	100	Royal James (Sandwich, Ad.)	100
Foudroyant	70	St Michael	90	Henry	82
Grand	70	Victory	82	Edgar	72
Tonnant	58	Royal Katherine	82	Rupert	66
Brave	54	Cambridge	70	Mountagu	62
Aquilon	50	Monmouth	66	Leopard	54
Duc	50	Dreadnought	62	Princess	54
Oriflamme	50	Fairfax	60	Mary Rose	48
Excellent	50	Yarmouth	54	Crown	48
Eole	38	Adventure	44	Success	32
Arrogant	38	Phoenix	42		
Superbe (des Rabinières, C.d'escadre)	70	Royal Charles (Harman, R.Ad.)	96	Sovereign (Jordan, V.Ad.)	100
Invincible	70	Rainbow	64	Triumph	70
Sans-Pareil	66	York	60	Unicorn	64
Fort	60	Anne	58	Mary	62
Sage	50	Greenwich	54	Plymouth	60
Heureux	50	Advice	48	Ruby	48
Rubis	46	Dover	48	Tiger	44
Galant	46	Forester	38		
Hardy	38				
30 ships – 1,664 guns		28 ships – 1,738 guns		24 ships – 1,540 guns	

The Dutch Fleet

Van Squadron		Centre Squadron		Rear Squadron	
Walcheren (Banckert, L.Ad.Z.)	70	Zeven Provincien (de Ruyter, C. in C.)	80	Dolfijn (van Gent, L.Ad.A)	82
Zierikzee (Evertsen, V.Ad.Z.)	60	Eendracht(A.van Nes, L.Ad.M.)	76	Oliphant (Sweers, V.Ad.A.)	82
Groeningen (Star, V.Ad.V.)	70	Maagd van Dordrecht (de Liefde, V.Ad.M.)	68	Pacificatie (Schramm, V.Ad. NQ.)	76
Oranje (Matthyszoon, SbN.Z.)	70	Ridderschap(J. van Nes, SbN.M.)	66	Gouda (de Haen, SbN.A.)	72
Prins Hendrik Casimir (Bruynsvelt, SbN.V.)	72	Westvriesland	78	Wapen van Enkhuisen (Vlugh, SbN.NQ.)	72
Zevenwolden	76	Reigersbergen	72	Komeetster	70
Oudshoorn	70	Waesdorp	68	Woerden	70
Kalandsoog	70	Stad Utrecht	66	Justina van Nassau	64
Steenbergen	64	Gelderland	64	Akerboom	60
Wapen van Nassau	62	Alkmaar	62	Amsterdam	60
Oostergo	62	Delft	62	Oosterwijk	60
Schieland	61	Wapen van Hoorn	62	Noorderkwartier	60
Kruiningen	56	Groot Hollandia	60	Gideon	58
Gelderland	56	Prov. van Utrecht	60	Essen	50
Steden	54	Deventer	60	Leeuwen	50
Middelburg	50	Westergo	56	Dordrecht	50
Kampveere	50	Wassenaar	50	Stavoren	48
Drie Helden Davids	50	Josua	54	Caleb	48
Vlissingen	50	Agatha	50	Jupiter	40
Wapen van Medemblik	46	Beschermer	50	Asperen	30
Zwanenburg	44	Jaarsveld	48	Overijssel	30
Delft	34	Zeelandia	44	Harderwijk	24
Ter Goes	34	Utrecht	36	Haas	24
Popkensberg	24	Windhond	34	Bommel	24
Schiedam	20	Brak	24		
		Postiljon	24		

Van Squadron	Centre Squadron	Rear Squadron
21 ships – 1,262 guns	22 ships – 1,362 guns	19 ships – 1,222 guns
4 frigates – 112 guns	4 frigates – 118 guns	5 frigates – 132 guns

Appendix III

The Fleets at Schooneveld

The Allied Fleet

Red Squadron		White Squadron		Blue Squadron	
London (Harman, V.Adm.)	96	*Terrible* (Des Ardents, Chef d'Escadre)	70	*St Michael* (Ossory, R.Adm	90
French Ruby	80	*Sans Pareil*	64	*Rainbow*	64
Resolution	70	*Conquérant*	56	*York*	60
Warspite	70	*Téméraire*	52	*Greenwich*	54
Triumph	70	*Précieux*	50	*Foresight*	48
Anne	58	*Aquilon*	50	*Hampshire*	46
Happy Return	54	*Prince*	50	*Sweepstakes*	42
Stavoreen	48	*Sage*	50		
Constant Warwick	42	*Oriflamme*	50		
Royal Charles (Rupert, Adm.)	100	*Reine* (d'Estrées,V.Adm.)	104	*Prince* (Spragge, Adm.)	100
Royal Katherine	82	*Invincible*	70	*Sovereign*	100
Henry	82	*Foudroyant*	70	*St George*	70
Edgar	72	*Tonnant*	64	*Cambridge*	70
Old James	70	*Glorieux*	64	*Dreadnought*	62
Rupert	66	*Excellent*	60	*Henrietta*	62
Lion	62	*Fier*	58	*Dunkirk*	60
Gloucester	62	*Aimable*	56	*Advice*	48
Princess	50	*Vaillant*	52		
Crown	48	*Apollon*	50		
Charles (Chicheley, R.Adm.)	96	*Orgueilleux* (de Grancey Chef d'Escadre)	70	*St Andrew* (Kempthorne, V.Adm.)	96
Victory	82	*Illustre*	70	*Unicorn*	64
Revenge	62	*Grand*	70	*Mary*	62
Newcastle	54	*Fortuné*	60	*Monk*	60
Yarmouth	54	*Bon*	52	*Diamond*	48
Mary Rose	48	*Bourbon*	52	*Ruby*	48
Assurance	42	*Duc*	50	*Bonaventure*	48
		Maure	50	*Falcon*	42
26 ships – 1,734 guns		27 ships – 1,624 guns		23 ships – 1,454 guns	

The Dutch Fleet

Van Squadron		Centre Squadron		Rear Squadron	
Gouden Leeuw (Tromp, L.Adm.A.)	82	Zeven Provincien (de Ruyter, C. in C.)	80	Walcheren (Banckert,L. Adm.Z.)	70
Pacificatie (Schram, V.Adm.NQ.)	80	Eendracht (A. van Nes, L.Adm.M.)	72	Zierikzee (Evertsen, V.Adm.Z.)	60
Hollandia (de Haen, SbN.A.)	80	Vrijheid (de Liefde, V.Adm.M.)	80	Wapen van Enkhuisen (Vlugh, SbN.NQ.)	72
Kalandsoog	70	Maagd van Dordrecht (J. van Nes, SbN.M.)	68	Westvriesland	78
Delft	62	Spiegel	70	Eenhoorn	70
Wassenaar	60	Steenburgen	70	Komeetster	70
Schieland	60	Waesdorp	68	Ridderschap	65
Amsterdam	60	Stad Utrecht	66	Justina van Nassau	65
Provincien van Utrecht	60	Deventer	66	Akerboom	62
Geloof	56	Alkmaar	64	Gideon	62
Prins te Paard	54	Prins	64	Domburg	60
Agatha	50	Gelderland	63	Noorderkwartier	60
Zuiderhuis	48	Beschermer	50	Gelderland	60
Wapen van Holland	46	Essen	50	Wapen van Nassau	58
Wakende Kraan	44	Caleb	46	Tijdverdrijf	56
Zeelandia	44	Dordrecht	44	Leeuwen	50
Jupiter	42	Wapen van Medemblik	44	Ter Veere	48
		Zeeland	42		
17 ships – 998 guns		18 ships – 1,107 guns		17 ships – 1,066 guns	

Appendix IV

The Fleets at the Texel

The Allied Fleet

There exists considerable uncertainty about the actual composition of the Allied fleet at the Battle of the Texel. It has been generally accepted that it consisted of about 90 ships of the line, and that 30 of these were French. Anderson concludes that if there were 60 English ships in the line of battle, that number must include at least three fifth rates. In his analysis of the fleet he continues:

> Even for the White or French Squadron, now back in its natural place in the van, it is impossible to give more than a general list. It contained the same 27 ships as at Schooneveld with the addition of the *Royale Thérèse* 100, *Pompeux* 70, and *Diamant* 54, and had thus 30 ships and 1,828 guns. The Marquis Martel in the *Royale Thérèse* commanded its first division as Rear Admiral, d'Estrées commanded the second and des Ardents the third.
>
> Among the English ships the following can be ascribed with fair certainty to either the Red or the Blue squadron, but not necessarily to particular divisions:
>
> Red Squadron: *Sovereign* (F.1), *London* (F.2), *Charles* (F.3), *Royal Katherine*, *Henry*, *Victory*, *French Ruby*, *Edgar*, *Warspite*, *Old James*, *Triumph*, *Resolution*, *Rupert*, *Monmouth*, *Mary*, *Crown*, *Advice*, and *Pearl*.
>
> Blue squadron: *Prince* (F.1), *Royal Charles*, *St Andrew* (F.2), *St Michael* (F.3), *Cambridge*, *Swiftsure* (3), *St George*, *Unicorn*, *Rainbow* (3), *Henrietta*, *Dreadnought*, *York* (3), *Lion*, *Gloucester*, *Dunkirk*, *Monck*, *Greenwich* (3), *Bristol*, *Bonaventure*, *Ruby*, *Hampshire* (3), *Portsmouth* (3), *Foresight* (3), *Sweepstakes* (3), *Success*, and *Guernsey*. The remaining ships were: *Fairfax*, *Plymouth*, *Anne*, *Happy Return*, *Princess*, *Newcastle*, *Yarmouth*, *Leopard*, *Nonsuch* (or *Portland*), *Stavoreen*, *Mary Rose*, *Diamond*, *Swallow*, *Assurance*, and *Falcon*.
>
> If my various guesses and suppositions are correct, the two English Squadrons – not counting the 5th Rates – consisted of 56 ships with 3,558 guns. Those of the Red Squadron were probably rather more powerful on an average than those of the Blue; this was the case at Schooneveld and is confirmed amongst those ships which can be ascribed to a particular squadron. Probably the 29 ships of the

Red carried about 1,870 guns and the 27 of the Blue about 1,690. The total for the whole fleet would be 86 ships and 5,386 guns.[1]

The Dutch Fleet

Van Squadron		Centre Squadron		Rear Squadron	
Gouden Leeuw (Tromp, L.Adm.A.)	82	Zeven Provincien (de Ruyter, C. in C.)	80	Walcheren (Banckert, L.Adm.Z.)	70
Olifant (Sweers, V.Adm.A.)	82	Eendracht(A. van Nes, L.Adm.M,)	72	Zierikzee (Evertsen, V.Adm.Z.)	60
Hollandia (de Haen,SbN.A.)	80	Vrijheid (de Liefde, V.Adm.M.)	80	Groeningen (Star, V.Adm.Z.)	70
Pacificatie	80	Maagd van Dordrecht(J. van Nes, SbN.M.)	68	Prins Hendrik Casimir (Bruynsvelt, SbN.Z)	72
Kalandsoog	70				
Komeetster	70	Voorsichtigheid	84	Westvriesland	78
Akerboom	62	Spiegel	70	Wapen van Enkhuisen	72
Delft	62	Steenbergen	70	Eenhoorn	70
Wassenaar	60	Waesdorp	68	Oostergo	68
Amsterdam	60	Stad Utrecht	66	Justina van Nassau	65
Noorderkwartier	60	Ridderschap	65	Prins	64
Prov. van Utrecht	60	Alkmaar	64	Gideon	62
Schieland	60	Gelderland	63	Domburg	60
Geloof	56	Beschermer	50	Gelderland	60
Prins te Paard	54	Essen	50	Wapen van Nassau	58
Agatha	50	Caleb	46	Tijdverdrijf	56
Zuiderhuis	48	Dordrecht	44	Steden	54
Wapen van Holland	46	Wapen van Medemblik	44	Leeuwen	50
Wakende Kraan	44	Zeeland	42	Vlissingen	50
Zeelandia	44			Dordrecht	50
Jupiter	42			Ter Veere	48
				Utrecht	42
21 ships – 1,272 guns		18 ships – 1,126 guns		21 ships – 1,269 guns	

Anderson notes that this list includes only ships of more than 40 guns; and remarks on the most unusual arrangement whereby de Ruyter's squadron was smaller than the others.[2]

---

1   Anderson, *Third Dutch War*, pp.402–403.
2   *Ibid.*, pp.402–403.

Bibliography

Anderson, R.C., *Journals and Narratives of the Third Dutch War* (Greenwich, London: Navy Records Society, 1946)

Anderson, R.C. (ed.) *The Journal of Edward Montagu, First Earl of Sandwich* (London: Navy Records Society, 1929)

Bamber, Michael, *General-at-Sea: Robert Blake and the Seventeenth-Century Revolution in Naval Warfare* (London: J. Murray, 1989)

Beadon, Roger, *Robert Blake* (London: Edward Arnold, 1935)

Blok, P., *The Life of Admiral de Ruyter*, trans. G.J. Renier (London: E. Benn, 1933)

Boxer, C.R., *The Dutch Seaborne Empire 1600-1800* (London: Penguin, 1965)

Bruijn, Jaap R., *The Dutch Navy of the Seventeenth and Eighteenth Centuries* (Columbia, South Carolina: University of South Carolina Press, 1990)

Capper, D.P., *Moat Defensive: A History of the Waters of the Nore Command, 55 BC to 1961* (London: A. Baker, 1963)

Clowes, William L., *The Royal Navy: A History From the Earliest Times to the Present*, 7 vols. (London: Sampson Low, Marston and Company, 1898)

Corbett, Julian S., *Fighting Instructions 1530–1816* (London: Conway Maritime Press, 1905)

Corbett, Julian S., *Monk* (London: Macmillan and Co., 1889)

Corbett, Julian S., *Views of the Battles of the Third Dutch War* (London: Navy Records Society, 1898)

Davies, J.D., *Pepys's Navy* (Barnsley: Seaforth Publishing, 2008)

Fox, Frank L., *Great Ships: The Battlefleet of King Charles II* (Greenwich, London: Conway Maritime Press, 1980)

Fox, Frank L., *The Four Days' Battle of 1666* (Barnsley: Seaforth Publishing, 2009)

Gardiner, Samuel R. and Atkinson, C.T. (eds.), *Letters and Papers Relating to the First Dutch War*, 4 vols. (London: Navy Records Society, 1899)

Hainsworth, Roger and Churches, Christine, *The Anglo-Dutch Naval Wars 1652–1674* (Stroud: Sutton, 1998)

Hattendorf, Professor J.B. et al. (eds,), *British Naval Documents 1204–1960* (Aldershot: Scolar Press, 1993)

Hornstein, Sari R., *The Restoration Navy and English Foreign Trade 1674–1688* (Aldershot: Scolar Press, 1991)

Jenkins, E.H., *A History of the French Navy* (London: Macdonald and Jane, 1973)

Jones, Professor J.R., *The Anglo-Dutch Wars of the Seventeenth Century* (London: Routledge, 1996)

Kirsch, Peter, *Fireship* (Barnsley: Seaforth Publishing, 2009)

Kitson, Frank, *Prince Rupert: Admiral and General-at-Sea* (London: Constable, 1998)

Konstam, Angus, *Warships of the Anglo-Dutch Wars* (Oxford: Osprey, 2011)

Konstam, Angus, *Sovereigns of the Sea* (Hoboken, New Jersey: J. Wiley & Sons, 2008)

Mahan, Alfred T., *The Influence of Sea Power Upon History* (Boston, Mass.: Little, Brown, and Co., 1894)

Marcus, G.J., *A Naval History of England*, 2 vols. (Boston, Mass.: Little, Brown and Co., 1961)

Ollard, Richard, *Clarendon and his Friends* (Oxford: Oxford University Press, 1987)

Ollard, Richard, *Cromwell's Earl: A Life of Edward Mountagu, 1st Earl of Sandwich* (London: Harper Collins, 1994)

Ollard, Richard, *Man of War: Sir Robert Holmes and the Restoration Navy* (London: Hodder and Stoughton, 1969)

Ollard, Richard, *Pepys* (Oxford: Oxford University Press, 1984)

Padfield, Peter, *Tide of Empire*, 3 vols. (London: Routledge and Kegan Paul, 1982)

Richmond, Admiral Sir Herbert, *The Navy as an Instrument of Policy 1558–1727* (Cambridge: Cambridge University Press, 1953)

Rodger, Professor N.A.M., *The Command of the Ocean* (London: Penguin, 2004)

Rogers, Colonel H.C.B., *Generals-at Sea: naval operations during the English Civil War and the three Anglo-Dutch wars* (Bromley: Galago, 1992)

Rogers, P.G., *The Dutch in the Medway* (London: C. Knight, 1970)

Shomette, Donald G., and Haslach, Robert D., *Raid on America* (Columbia, South Carolina: University of South Carolina, 1988)

Spencer, Charles, *Prince Rupert: The Last Cavalier* (London: Weidenfeld and Nicolson, 2007)

Tanner, J.R. (ed.), *Samuel Pepys's Naval Minutes* (London: Navy Records Society, 1976)

Tedder, A.W., *The Navy of the Restoration* (Cambridge: Cornmarket Press, 1916)

Tomalin, Claire, *Samuel Pepys: The Unequalled Self* (London: Penguin, 2012)

Uglow, Jenny, *A Gambling Man* (London: Faber and Faber, 2009)

Van der Moer, Abraham, 'Michiel Adriaenszoon de Ruyter' in *The Great Admirals*, ed. Jack Sweetman (Annapolis, MD: Naval Institute Press, 1997)

Worner. Oliver, *Hero of the Restoration A Life of General George Monck, 1st Duke of Albemarle, K.G.* (London: Jarrolds, 1936)

Weygand, General Max, *Turenne: Marshal of France* (London: Houghton Mifflin Co., 1930)

Wheeler, James Scott, *The Making of a World Power: war and the military revolution in seventeenth-century England* (Stroud: Sutton, 1999)

Wilcox, L.A., *Mr Pepys's Navy* (London: G. Bell, 1966)